Forever 19

Kaye S. Beechum

WESTBOW
PRESS®
A DIVISION OF THOMAS NELSON
& ZONDERVAN

WestBow Press books may be ordered through booksellers or by contacting:

WestBow Press
A Division of Thomas Nelson & Zondervan
1663 Liberty Drive
Bloomington, IN 47403
www.westbowpress.com
1 (866) 928-1240

ISBN: 978-1-5127-1964-2 (sc)
ISBN: 978-1-5127-1965-9 (hc)
ISBN: 978-1-5127-1963-5 (e)

Library of Congress Control Number: 2015918871

Print information available on the last page.

WestBow Press rev. date: 11/10/2015

Contents

Acknowledgments xi

Introduction xiii

Chapter 1 The Accident 1

Chapter 2 In the Hospital 9

Chapter 3 Birth and Infancy 15

Chapter 4 Childhood 21

Chapter 5 Tween and Teen Years 43

Chapter 6 The Young Woman 55

Chapter 7 Saying Good-Bye 69

Chapter 8 Grieving 75

Chapter 9 Cheryl's Final Gift 81

Chapter 10 Memories of Cheryl 87

To George, Gordon, and Coral Joy, my three loving, unique, and special children, who have waited a very long time for me to put this story on paper.

Farewell beloved child! The bright eternal doors have closed after thee, we shall see thy sweet face no more. Oh, woe for them who watched thy entrance into heaven, when they shall wake and find only the cold gray sky of daily life, and thou gone forever!

—Harriet Beecher Stowe, *Uncle Tom's Cabin*

Acknowledgments

There are three people without whose help this book may never have been completed—my daughter, Coral Joy; her son, Geoffrey; and a young lady, Sara, whom we think of as a family member (and hopefully she will be one day). Each of these individuals used his or her special talents to supplement my meager writing skills.

Coral read, reread, made suggestions, and helped with memories almost forgotten as we worked closely on developing and completing this book. We spent many hours reminiscing, sharing stories, and crying together. Even after all these years, the pain of loss for both of us was ever present. I am so grateful she was willing and able to help me bring my dream to completion.

Geoffrey has an artistic bent, which he seldom has time to express. He was only three years old when we lost his auntie Cheryl, and he never got to know her very well. She loved him dearly and would be so pleased to know he drew such a loving sketch of her. I was happy when he agreed to do this, as he felt he might not do her justice. He did just fine.

Sara is a special friend of another son of Coral's, Greg. Sara and Greg are "computer nerds" and work well together. Sara's specialty is graphics, and I asked her whether she could assist with preparing all the images and photos to the particular specifications required by the publisher. She did so happily.

I participate in a weekly creative writing workshop, and I would be remiss if I did not thank the entire group for their encouragement as I struggled and worked on developing my writing skills.

My deepest thanks to everyone who has helped me make this book possible.

Introduction

My daughter Cheryl Jean has been gone for many years, and although it has been something I have wanted to do for a long time, until now I have been unable to share her story. In the beginning, her loss was too painful for me to talk about. Everywhere I went and everything I did brought forth memories of her. A song we both enjoyed or a trip we took together; these things kept her memory painfully in the forefront. I often even imagined I saw her, when it was merely someone who looked just like her driving by or walking down the street. Painful as it was, I did not want to forget her either. I wanted in some way to keep her alive. The pain has subsided with the passing years, and I feel now is the time to share these memories and feelings. I realize she was not the first young woman to lose her life in a car accident, and I certainly was not the first mother to lose a child. Perhaps in the sharing of Cheryl's life and the telling of how her family and friends dealt with her death, I will be able to help others who have faced a similar loss, and maybe that will help me to put my loss into perspective.

This is the story of a promising life cut short. A story of a beautiful girl—daughter, granddaughter, sister, niece, aunt, and friend. She was so bubbly and outgoing, so full of life. She was a happy person who had big plans for her future. She was loving, dedicated, talented, imaginative, creative, emotional, wild, and crazy. As I am writing this, I feel a profound emptiness. I realize by calendar years that my younger daughter, Cheryl Jean, would now, in 2015, be fifty years old. But when I think of her, I can only picture the bright and lively nineteen-year-old girl who was poised on the threshold of her life.

Cheryl Jean had a truly beautiful soul, and everyone loved her. She earned many nicknames in her life, but the one that really stuck was Bug. She was a lover of cats and a champion of underdogs. She wanted to fix everybody and everything. She was like every other nineteen-year-old and yet nothing like any other person in the world. She was my baby, and this is her story.

The family misses her so much, especially her older sister, Coral Joy, and me. When we spend time together, we find ourselves frequently wondering what it would be like to have Cheryl there with us. When we go somewhere or do something special, one of us might be heard to say, "Cheryl would love this" or "I wonder what Cheryl would think of this." Even though we may have come to terms with her absence, there is still a hole in our family where Cheryl should be.

The family has always made an effort to keep Cheryl's memory alive. All her nieces and nephews, even those who were born long after she left us, are told stories about her. This is just one way we keep her memory alive. At special family meals, such as Christmas or Thanksgiving, we still set a place at the table where she would sit if she were there. When her birthday rolls around, we think about her and sometimes reminisce about her. The hardest time for me is always the month of August because that is the month in which she had her accident and subsequently died. I try to put the memories out of my mind and think about other things, but I often suddenly feel a great depression, and only then will I realize what date it is.

Lately, however, I have been able to think back, piece it all together, and write it down so she will always be remembered.

1

The Accident

It was three years before I came out of the fog I was in. I wasn't counting days or months; I was just surviving. I was putting one foot in front of the other, and I was trying to do what had to be done, trying to fill the void, trying to avoid the pain. I didn't even know that I had been in a fog until it began to clear away. Now all that is left of the original pain is a vague ache, an empty spot in my soul, and so many beautiful memories of a happy child, a beautiful young woman who left us much too soon.

Sometimes I wake up in the middle of the night, and I remember; I see her curly blonde hair streaming down over her shoulders, her sparkling blue eyes. I see her happy smile. I can almost hear her say, "Hi, Mommy." Even at nineteen years old she still called me Mommy! Not always, and certainly not in front of her friends, but just between us. I may not really hear her voice, but I do feel her presence at times, even after all these years.

At first I didn't have many dreams of her. It's been so many years since she died, and I've dreamed of her only a handful of times. I expected to dream of her soon after she died, and I waited for the experience, but it didn't come right away. When my dad died, I had dreams about him for two or three years afterward, and I still do sometimes. These dreams did not come often, but they were very real. I would dream that he was alive, and the context would be "Oh, Dad, I thought you were dead, and you're not! I am so glad you have come back to us!" The dreams felt so real, and I would wake up feeling so emotional. The feeling would stay sometimes for days.

I have had only a few real dreams about Cheryl, and they were far apart. In the first one, I was outside, possibly on a beach, and there was a long walkway or sidewalk. It was very foggy, and I saw a blonde girl off in the distance walking away from me on this walkway. Soon I realized it was Cheryl, and I called to her and tried to reach her, but I could not, and she kept moving farther away. I may have dreamed this more than once, but I think not. Later I had another dream. The only thing I remember about it is that, just before I woke up, I saw Cheryl's face right up close to mine. She was angry, and she said very clearly, "I hate you!" That really shook me up. I have no idea why I dreamed it. Was I feeling guilty about something between us? Or was she coming to me in a dream to voice this feeling? More recently I have had dreams in which she was up close but didn't recognize me or respond to me. I have had a few dreams in which family members talked as if she was alive but had left home and wasn't coming back, and I couldn't find her to communicate with her. I don't know what these dreams have meant, if anything. I keep thinking—hoping, really—that I have had so few dreams because there was nothing unresolved between us, so she let go and moved on.

Before I begin piecing my story together, I should provide a little background. I worked for the Los Angeles Police Department in the Parking and Traffic Management Section. I had been heavily involved in the traffic planning for the 1984 Los Angeles Summer Olympics over the previous few years, and it all boiled down to two weeks of twelve-hour days to bring it all together. While I was busy with this, Cheryl, who had been attending Harbor Junior College, was enjoying her summer vacation by visiting some of the Olympic venues.

When the 1984 Summer Olympics were over, I found myself back in the office trying to get back to normal; Cheryl had just begun working at a new job. I was sitting at my desk on August 22 when I received a phone call. The caller identified herself and asked if I owned a silver Mazda. I acknowledged that I did. She said not to worry but asked whether I knew someone named Cheryl. From then on, everything became a haze. The caller said that Cheryl had been in an accident and was in Daniel Freeman Hospital in Inglewood. The caller repeated that I was not to worry but that she needed to talk with me, asking whether I could go there.

Being told not to worry but to come right away made me feel that something was dreadfully wrong. I quickly hung up the phone and immediately realized I didn't know how to get there, so I called back and asked for directions. I don't even remember how I found the phone number, but I did. Then, as calmly as I could, I got up from my desk and began walking out of the office. Several people had overheard my side of the conversation. Even though I felt I had been speaking quietly and calmly, they must have known it was something serious because there were offers to drive me, but I refused them. I had my own car and felt capable of driving myself. I believed I was keeping it together very well.

I was so calm I didn't even remember to tell my supervisor I was leaving. I did call my older son, George, at home just before I left work. I told him his sister had been in an accident and asked him to meet me at the hospital. It was about a half-hour drive from downtown Los Angeles where I worked to Inglewood where the hospital was, and all the way there I drove as carefully as I could, all the while trying desperately to calm the mounting fear that was trying to overcome me. I kept praying over and over, and part of what I prayed was "Please, Lord, don't let it be head injuries. Please don't let it be her face." I don't know why the thought of head injuries came to me. Perhaps it was because the caller had said that Cheryl was not able to talk with her at the moment, and my natural assumption then was that she was unconscious. To me, being unconscious meant head injuries, very bad head injuries!

Cheryl had been taken to Daniel Freeman Hospital, which at the time was a Catholic institution; it has since been closed down. When I arrived at the emergency room, George was already there waiting for me because home was much closer to Inglewood than my office was. We had to wait a short while before we were taken in to speak with a nun. That was when I was told that Cheryl had been involved in a very serious traffic accident in which the car she was driving had rolled over. She had sustained major head injuries in the accident, and she was being given only a fifty-fifty chance to survive. She needed immediate surgery to relieve the pressure on her brain. I was allowed to see her for only a few minutes before they rushed her into surgery. When I saw my beautiful girl, her lovely blonde hair had all been shaved off, and she was attached to several machines. She was unresponsive, but I don't think that I noticed any of that. It was when I touched her hand that I finally broke down and cried.

Later I learned the details of the accident. Cheryl had been running an errand on her lunch break. She was driving the car that I had just given her so she would have transportation to her new job. According to the accident report from the Torrance Police Department, she had been driving eastbound on Manhattan Beach Boulevard in Torrance at a speed of about thirty miles per hour. She struck a vehicle from behind, and her car spun around and flipped over. The car she struck was waiting in the number-two driving lane to make a right turn into a driveway, and she didn't see him in time to stop. Cheryl had not been wearing her seat belt at the time of the accident, and that is the reason she sustained such serious head injuries. I have no idea why she was not wearing her seat belt that day; it was something that we had discussed at length, and I had always been adamant about the seriousness of wearing it at all times. Besides the head injuries, Cheryl just had a broken wrist and some bruises. I can only wonder what the outcome of the accident would have been if she had been wearing her seat belt.

After the surgery, Cheryl was taken to the trauma unit. She was in a coma, and all there was for me to do was wait and gather the family. My second son, Gordon, was living with my mother in Salinas at the time, so I called Mom. She and Gordon came as quickly as they could get a flight. Mom took the news calmly enough, but Gordon kept saying to me, "Don't let her die." I didn't know what to say because, of course, I had no control over the outcome, so I just told him to pray. Getting in touch with my older daughter, Coral Joy, was not as easy. She had very recently moved out of state, and I did not yet have her new phone number or address. This was before the days when everyone carried a phone with them. I knew that she was in Idaho living with relatives of her husband, but that was all I knew. I was at a loss as to how to contact her.

From the moment they put Cheryl in the trauma unit, I stayed at the hospital. There was a tiny waiting room across the hall from the trauma unit where I slept and ate when I could. I had no intention of leaving, as I needed to be near Cheryl. In the beginning, George would drive back and forth from home, bringing me what I needed so I didn't have to leave. My coworkers and friends at the police department were very helpful. A detective asked if there was anything he could do to help, and what I really needed at that moment was to find my other daughter. The only thing I knew was that her mother-in-law worked for the county of Los Angeles. So I gave the detective her name and asked if he could get in touch with her and find out how I could get a message to my daughter. The detective took his partner with him and went to her office. Being police officers they, of course, questioned her as if she was a suspect. This was not really a negative thing; it just came as second nature to them. She was quite upset, and she didn't tell the officers anything, but she got the number of the waiting room where I was so she could call me.

When she called, she told me that she wasn't very happy that I had sent the police to her office. She felt they had interrogated her. I explained to her that I needed to talk with my daughter immediately, and she wouldn't even give me any information. So I told her that Cheryl had been in a horrible accident and was in a coma. She responded that she would call Coral Joy and give her the information and the phone number where she could contact me. When Coral Joy called, I told her what had happened, and of course, she wanted to come right away. She couldn't afford the plane fare from Idaho, so I arranged for that, and she took the first flight she could get. Mom had arrived quickly and was helping me a lot during this time. I don't know if she had driven my car or if George had driven her in my car, but she was able to get to the airport and get an airplane ticket sent to Coral Joy and subsequently meet her when she arrived. So for a couple of days, I was there at the hospital with all my children together. Our family sat vigil for Cheryl in that little waiting room across the hall from the trauma unit. We cried, prayed, and reminisced. Cheryl lay in a coma fighting for her life.

2

In the Hospital

Gordon couldn't stay at the hospital with us as long as I would have liked. Mom needed him to return to Salinas to work in the liquor store that she owned. She couldn't afford for both of them to be away for an extended period of time, and we had no way of knowing how long Cheryl would remain in the coma. This was a good thing for him because he was having an extremely hard time dealing with the situation, and I knew going home and getting back to work would be just the thing to take his mind off of what was happening in the hospital with his little sister.

In my mind, time stood still for the days my family and I sat vigil in that hospital. It had all happened so quickly—in just one week—and yet time dragged too. Cheryl had been in a coma since the accident, and then on the third day she awoke briefly. At this point we became very hopeful. She couldn't see us because her eyes were bandaged; she couldn't speak due to all the tubes in her mouth. They had shaved off all her beautiful blonde hair, and her head was swathed in bandages. She was attached to all sorts of machines; it was such a devastating sight. Family members could visit her only one at a time and then only for a few minutes. The nurses would let me stay a bit longer, and I would just sit by her bed and hold her hand. Sometimes I would talk to her, but I was in such a numb state that I didn't know what to say. Afterward, I have thought and thought and wondered if maybe I should have sung to her, or maybe I should have said inspirational and optimistic things to her. Perhaps I could have encouraged her to fight for her life. But then again, would any of that have made a difference? I will never know. She would squeeze my hand from time to time very softly, sometimes seemingly in response to something I had said. I even asked her if she knew what had happened, and she sort of shook her head no. Then she slipped back into the coma. That was the only time that she came out of the coma, and it was for only a few hours on that third day after the accident.

We spent the entire week in the hospital, waiting, hoping, praying. Our world was the trauma unit and that tiny waiting room. My memories of that time are mostly blurred, but a few things stand out clearly in my mind. On the first day of our vigil, Cheryl's new boss came to see me. She had just received news of the accident, and I had no idea who had contacted her. She was very concerned for Cheryl. She told me that, although Cheryl had worked for her only for a short time, she really liked her and expressed what a hard worker Cheryl was. She also explained to me that, since Cheryl was on her lunch break when the accident occurred, she couldn't file a worker's compensation claim. I don't know why she felt the need to share that piece of information at that particular moment when Cheryl's life was hanging in the balance. At that time anything except what was happening in the hospital was the last thing on my mind. I just needed Cheryl to wake up, and then I could think about what came next. I also remember sitting there and going through Cheryl's purse. Someone had asked me for some information that would be found in the purse, and I couldn't find it even though I went through her things over and over. At some point someone took pity on me, took the purse from me, and found what I was looking for. She found it quite easily. The staff members of that hospital were very considerate and good at their jobs.

During our time at the hospital, we had the opportunity to get to know the nurses who took care of Cheryl. They were such patient and hardworking people. They worked twelve-hour shifts in the trauma unit. Each day they were assigned to a different patient, so we got to know most of the nurses who worked in that unit. We were told they were rotated so that they would not get attached to any one patient. I am sure this was done primarily for the nurses' emotional well-being. As caring as they were, I am sure they had a tendency to get emotionally involved with their patients. They would also periodically be rotated out of the trauma unit, as it was a very difficult assignment. Of all the nurses we met, there are only two who stand out in my memory. One was a buxom, matronly woman. She was very kind and tender to the patients and sort of motherly to the family members. The other one was a young woman who went about her work very precisely and was not really friendly to the family members at all, just very businesslike. I don't recall ever seeing her smile. We called her "the ice maiden." We later discovered this was a shell she had developed for her own emotional protection, as she actually fell into Coral Joy's arms and cried when she was told that Cheryl had died. I couldn't imagine doing the job of a trauma unit nurse; I had great admiration for these women.

In the week we spent in the hospital, several of Cheryl's friends came to see her. I don't remember how many or who they were, but I remember thinking that my daughter was greatly loved. Since only family members were allowed in to the trauma unit to see Cheryl, her friends would sit and talk with us. They would attempt to cheer me with stories of Cheryl and by expressing their feelings about her. Diana, one of her closest friends, came to visit and brought a little stuffed animal as a gift. When she found out she couldn't go in to see Cheryl, she gave it to me. She wanted me to give it to Cheryl when she woke up, but of course this was never to be. I still have this little mouse, and today when I look at it, the memories are easier to handle.

Cheryl had always been a doting aunt to her big sister's two little boys; often she would pick them up and take them with her on outings. She would always introduce them to her friends as "my boys." They were three and five years old at the time of her accident. It was bittersweet for me when one of her friends came to the hospital to pay his respects and asked me, "What is going to happen to her two sons?" The question stunned me for a moment until I realized he really thought they were her own children. He was very surprised when I explained that they were her nephews.

Many of the visitors were friends and coworkers of mine. I truly felt their caring concern as they came together offering their support and their prayers. One fellow from my office came more than once and sat with me discussing current projects we were working on, probably hoping to distract me a bit. He also became a sort of messenger between me and my supervisor regarding my use of vacation time and so on, because at this point I didn't even care if I lost pay or lost my job. Nothing was more important than the vigil I was keeping and my prayers for the life of my darling daughter. When it was all over, I knew I owed him a great deal of thanks for his help in that regard.

On the morning of August 29, exactly one week after the accident, I awoke with a feeling of dread that stayed with me all day. Coincidentally, this date was exactly four years to the day after I had lost a younger brother, and I truly believed that was where my feeling of dread originated. I remember thinking, *Lord, this time You have given me a mountain.* I guess it was a prayer of sorts. I was thinking I could not face what the day was going to bring, and I didn't really know yet what that was.

On that day, as on all the others, Mom tried to get me to go home. She wanted me to shower, eat, and rest, but as on every day for the last seven days, I could not bear to leave the hospital. Some of my coworkers came to visit me that day, as many had over the past few days. They asked what they could do for me, and I suggested going downstairs and giving blood in Cheryl's name. Several of them chose to do this, and George and Coral Joy did as well. While they were all off giving blood, I was very restless, so I chose to go down to the chapel to pray. Some of my friends went with me. One coworker, I remember, who was a professed Christian, prayed loudly, pounding his fist on the back of the pew and stating, "You can't take her, God! Don't You dare take this girl from us!" I can't even describe the pain I felt as he did this. It not only bothered me, but it angered me. It has always been my belief that we can ask God for things, but we can't order Him or make demands of Him. Whatever happens is His ultimate decision. I really preferred to sit quietly and meditate or pray silently. My plaintive prayer was "Lord, please let Cheryl live. Please take me instead." What mother wouldn't send up such a prayer? I would have surely welcomed a miracle, but none was forthcoming. Eventually, everyone left, and I was alone with my own thoughts and prayers.

I don't know how long I stayed in the chapel. It was so peaceful, and I needed that right at that time more than anything. After a while, I returned to the trauma waiting room, and I was told that the nurses had been looking for me. I knew that there had been a lot of activity in Cheryl's little cubicle that morning—nurses bustling about and changing machines—so I checked in with them hoping beyond hope that they would be able to give me some good news. What the nurses told me was that Cheryl had taken a turn for the worse, and they knew I would want to be with her then. So I went in to the trauma unit to Cheryl's little cubicle, sat down, and took hold of her hand. I looked at my beautiful daughter lying there in that hospital bed with all the tubes and wires connected to her and the machines humming beside the bed. I sat with her, and I held her hand, and I talked to her, and I kept talking to her even though I received no response. I was very focused on Cheryl, but at the same time vaguely aware of what was going on around me. The nurses were hurrying about providing care for the other trauma patients, and one nurse was on the phone talking about having a machine checked to ensure it was working. I later discovered that the particular machine she had been talking about was the one connected to my daughter, and the problem with it was that it showed no brain wave activity. I think the nurses wanted to believe that there was something wrong with the machine rather than that they were losing Cheryl. At any rate, they were taking every precaution to ensure the machine was accurate before taking any further steps. While I was sitting there with Cheryl, the nurses bustling around, my mind began to wander backward in time.

3

Birth and Infancy

When I was a young woman, my family lived in Salinas, California. We lived there to be near the Fort Ord military base, which was in Monterey, because my dad was stationed there. In early 1957, when I was nineteen, I met and married George, who was also nineteen. I was a waitress, and he was a handsome, charismatic soldier. It had been a whirlwind romance, and we became parents very quickly. Soon after our marriage, George was discharged from the army and decided to go to college, subsequently achieving an associate of arts degree. By 1960 our little family had grown to five. George and I now had three beautiful children, two boys and a girl. With the birth of our third child, George and I decided that we had the perfect-sized family, and we didn't plan to have any more children.

Shortly after our third child was born, we moved to Alexandria, Virginia, to be near George's family. We settled in pretty well. I got a job working for a telephone answering service, and George began working at United Airlines as a ramp agent. At first we lived in an apartment in town, but soon we were able to purchase a small house on the outskirts of town. After living there, seemingly happy and content, for almost three years, we began having marital problems. It seemed my husband was having an affair. After I found out about his little indiscretion, we talked it over, and he promised to stop, but when I discovered that he had broken his promise, I decided to leave him. Since he worked for United Airlines, I could travel for free on standby when seats were available, so I was able to take the three children and return to my family in Salinas, California.

Back in Salinas, my children and I stayed with my younger brother and his wife. I got a job as a waitress at the Pancake House where my dad, now retired from the army, was the manager. My children and I began settling in to start a new life. When I had been in Salinas for just a few months, George arranged a transfer so he could work at San Francisco International Airport. He came to me in Salinas and said he wanted to reconcile. He promised the affair he had been having really was over, and he was very contrite and convincing. I felt strongly that the children needed their father, so I relented and agreed to make another go at the marriage. We moved to San Mateo, which was near the San Francisco Airport, and began to work on mending our marriage. Not very long after that, I found out that I was pregnant again. This was upsetting to me, and this time I was not pleased. I had hoped to stop at three children. I really had no plans for having more children, and George and I were still struggling to keep our marriage together. I didn't think it was a good idea at all to bring another child into our family at this time. I constantly struggled with these negative feelings. How could I feel this way about the child growing within me?

I continued to struggle with these feelings as my pregnancy progressed. The turning point for me came when a family tragedy occurred. My brother and his wife lost their three-month-old daughter, Kimberly Ann, to sudden infant death syndrome (SIDS). This was their first child, and this was the first major tragedy to be experienced by our family. The baby died the day after my family had gathered at my apartment to give me a baby shower. My mom and other family members had driven up to San Mateo from Salinas for the day to give me this shower. Kimberly Ann was such a sweet little baby, and my three children, George, Gordon, and Coral Joy, had been very taken with her. They wanted to play with her and hold her, but she was only three months old, and I told them to just look at her and talk to her, but not to touch her. As I recall, one of us had a cold, and I was worried about giving it to the baby. Kimberly Ann died unexpectedly the day after the shower. My mom had been caring for her at the time. Upon hearing the news of Kimberly Ann's death, I suddenly realized how blessed I was, and I thanked God for my three lovely children. I now earnestly embraced the new life within me. My dad had waited a day or two before calling me with the news; he was very worried about how it would affect me because of my pregnancy. I have never been the hysterical kind of person, so while he was telling me, I just listened and then tried to say all the comforting things I could think of. But when the call was over, I immediately went into the bedroom where my own three precious children were sleeping and checked them all to ensure they were breathing. This became a nightly ritual for me for many weeks to come. Often, when something bad happens to them, people pray to God and say, "Why me? What did I ever do to be punished this way?" I found myself praying a very different prayer. I found myself saying, "Why me, Lord? Why am I so fortunate that I have three strong, healthy children and another on the way when my brother has lost his only child?" At that time I could not even imagine how terribly painful it could be to lose a child. I worried for a long time that I might have a problem with my pregnancy because I had been so selfish as to wish that I was not pregnant.

At this point in time, I was six months along. By the time I was almost eight months along, I began experiencing problems. I was bleeding. Not a lot, just spotting, but it was frightening at any rate. The doctor told me I would be just fine if I went to bed and stayed there until it was time to deliver the baby. That, of course, was out of the question. There was no way, with three small children and a working husband, that I could just go to bed and stay there. We lived in an upstairs apartment, and I had to go downstairs to the laundry room to wash the clothes, which I did quite often having three active children, two of them boys. I was also babysitting two neighbor children at this time. I stopped that job right away. One cannot, however, stay in bed when three young children are running around the house and need feeding and caring for. Hiring a babysitter was out of the question, as money was always very tight. To compound the problem, my husband did not believe that the doctor had told me to stay in bed; he thought I was just being lazy. Needless to say, I did not take to my bed for the duration. I did do my best to slow down as much as possible because by now I really feared losing this baby. One of our boys was in kindergarten and the other was in first grade, so I was able to get some rest during the day while they were at school.

And then my husband left me again! It seems that the woman he had been seeing in Virginia was also carrying his child, so he transferred back to Washington National Airport. He just left for work one day and didn't come home. When I called looking for him, his coworker told me about his transfer. Working for the airlines gave him quite a bit of flexibility; he had the ability to just pick up and leave. So I contacted my family, and they helped once again to move me and the children back to Salinas. I moved into a three-bedroom house that my dad owned and kept as a rental. Fortunately it was empty at that time. I lived there until Cheryl was born. My dad did not charge me any rent, and I don't remember what we did for food and expenses, but probably my family kicked in.

Cheryl Jean was born on March 3, 1965. She was the biggest of all my babies at eight pounds, three and a quarter ounces, and twenty inches long. And she was blonde—so blonde we had to look very closely to see that she had hair, including eyebrows and eyelashes. Right from the beginning, she was very different from her older siblings. The first three months were very difficult as she seemed to cry so much more than the others had. While she was crying, her father, who had returned to us once more, would look at her and say, "She looks like a buzzard!" He thought this was so funny, and he wanted to nickname her "Buzzard." The idea to name my beautiful little girl after an ugly vulture made me angry, so eventually the nickname was shortened to Bug, and that stuck. Her siblings liked it and called her that most of her life. From the beginning, she didn't make physical progress as quickly as her older siblings had. Cheryl didn't roll over, sit up, or stand holding on to things as quickly as I expected. After the first few months of almost constantly crying, she was content to just lie around enjoying the view and laughing.

I was very concerned at Cheryl's lack of progress; I couldn't take anything for granted as I had with my other three children. Kimberly Ann's death was still very much with me. I voiced my concerns to the pediatrician at Cheryl's regular checkups. As it turned out, she was just much heavier than the other children had been, and perhaps just a little bit lazy, so she didn't try all the new things that babies usually try early on. I remember trying to get her to sit up. I would sit her up, and she would just flop over onto her side and laugh. It was a fun game for her. When she should have been learning how to walk, she would just plop down on the floor and laugh—another fun game. I remember worrying about her physical strength, and I also worried she may not be very smart. My older children had all picked up everything so quickly, and comparing Cheryl to them I kept thinking, *How could there be nothing wrong with Cheryl?* Now as I look back at the baby book I kept for her, I see I made no mention of my worries in it, so perhaps it was not as bad as I remember, or perhaps I just didn't want to voice my concerns in writing. In any case, she was a very happy-go-lucky baby, a trait that stayed with her all the rest of her life.

4

Childhood

Shortly after Cheryl was born, my husband returned again and said he wanted to be a part of our lives once more. This was getting tedious, but since I still had no income of my own, and since the children loved their daddy very much and were so happy to see him again, I decided to take him back. This became an on-and-off thing for the next few years until I finally decided to really call it quits and divorce him. By the time this came to pass, I had a good job and was able to take care of my family on my own. Cheryl was four years old when her father and I divorced, so she basically grew up without a father in the home.

My family had become a handful by now; the boys were very active and rambunctious as normal boys usually are. Cheryl turned out to be a normal healthy child, but she was quite chubby, unlike her older siblings. The whole family sort of spoiled her since she was the baby of the family. Well, I should say her older siblings spoiled her when they weren't picking on her. Cheryl learned how to hold her own, though, and most of the time she just laughed it off. She quickly overcame her slow beginnings and was pretty smart in school, which was mainly due to the attentions of her sister, Coral Joy, who was four years older and who prided herself on teaching her little sister to read and learn. They used to play school together, and Coral Joy would be the teacher. I think the attention from her older sister prompted Cheryl's desire to learn, and that was good. I have always believed that children who are read to and who learn to read at a young age will develop a love of reading and become avid learners in school. I always read to my older children, but by the time I was raising Cheryl, I had become a single parent and was spending a lot of time working and caring for my family, so didn't have time to read to her as much as I had the other children.

As time went by, I do not recall being especially overprotective of Cheryl, even though as she grew she was quite accident prone and also became a little tomboy. She was tough and was able to hold her own in a fight. Being rough-and-tumble, she ran around the house like a little whirlwind, sometimes following one of her older siblings and sometimes just running for the fun of it. I remember once when Cheryl was two years old, she tripped over her own feet. This was nothing new, only this time she landed on her right hand and came away crying. She couldn't move it without a good deal of pain, and I was afraid she had broken her wrist. As it turned out, all the wrist bones had sort of squished together like the bellows of an accordion, as the doctor described it. There were no broken bones. It wasn't serious, and he put her arm in a sling to protect her hand until the little bones fell back into place. She, however, would not rest or keep her arm in the sling. She just laughed and ran around as usual. She eventually healed, but I am sure it took longer than it should have due to her refusal to calm down.

There was another incident when she was about four or five. She fell out of bed and broke her collarbone. She had come in to sleep with me because she'd had a bad dream. I was sleeping in a king-sized bed so there was lots of room, certainly plenty for me and one small child. As soon as she crawled in, she proceeded to take over the whole bed. I was lying on my side on the far left side of the bed, and she was cuddled up right next to my back, and we fell back to sleep lying this way. Suddenly I heard her screaming. She had fallen out of the bed clear over on the right-hand side. She began crying and hollering that I had pushed her out of bed, which of course I had not. To this day I don't know how it happened. I am sure she was as rambunctious asleep as she was awake. Anyway, as I said, she broke her collarbone, and once again I was supposed to keep her quiet and not let her run around and play. Right! That was like saying I should harness a cheetah and keep it from running around. The break eventually healed, even though there was no cast or anything to hold the break in place, but the experience didn't convince her to slow down, and she would always tease me about the time I pushed her out of bed.

Another fond memory … once when Cheryl was about three years old there was a knock at the front door. I opened it to find two young boys standing there. The older looked to be about twelve or so, and he was upset. In an angry voice, he said, "I want to see Cheryl!" So I called Cheryl to the door. When the older boy saw her, he looked at his younger brother and said, "*She* beat you up?" And he grabbed his brother and dragged him away. I think he had come over to defend his little brother against the big bully Cheryl and was really shocked to see a petite, curly-headed, sweet-faced little blond. I guess Cheryl really could do a little more than hold her own in a fight.

Off and on through the years, our family had pet dogs, but from a very young age, Cheryl was a cat person. At one point she even decided she didn't like dogs at all. This was after she was bitten by a stray dog that her father had found. After that incident, on occasion, she showed some fear of dogs, and she said she would always love cats best. When she was about four years old, her father gave her a female Siamese kitten. It was very beautiful as all Siamese cats are. She became extremely attached to this kitten and carried it around with her all the time. It was at this time that we found out that Cheryl was quite allergic to cats. This is also when I first learned how determined my little girl could be. Even though she knew that it was her little kitty that was making her sneeze, cough, and feel miserable, she refused to give it up. She was sure that her kitty would not do this to her on purpose! So she suffered through it, snuggling the kitten every day and sleeping with the kitten every night. Eventually her body grew used to the kitten. As the symptoms lessened, she was able to be around it without being miserable. This would become a pattern throughout her life every time she got a new cat.

One day when the family returned home from an outing, we discovered that her kitty was missing. For days on end her sister and brothers helped her to search for it. They knocked on doors and asked everyone they knew. Unfortunately, Siamese are a popular breed of cat, and I feared it had been stolen. When the kids, all excited, called me at work one day to announce they had found the kitten, I was so happy for her. Cheryl was trying to tell me on the phone where and how they had found her. She said, "I am sure it is her, but she has some funny little bumps on the end of her tail." I didn't realize what she meant until I arrived home that evening to discover that she had found a male kitten. She, of course, didn't know the difference. It took a lot of talking and explaining to convince her that this was not her kitty. I finally was able to get her to understand that she needed to return it to the yard where she had found it, as there was probably another little boy or girl very sad over the loss of his or her pet. Unfortunately, we never did find her kitty, and she never owned another Siamese cat.

There were two more cats in the family during Cheryl's childhood. Each was brought home by one of her siblings, but it didn't take Cheryl very long to adopt them as her own. The first was a little gray kitty that we had for only a couple of weeks, not even long enough to get attached to. Sadly, he was run over by a car in the driveway of our apartment complex. This was a bit traumatic for all the kids, and it was a while before we decided to have another cat. Then Coral Joy brought home a gray tabby when Cheryl was about nine years old. This was the most memorable of all our cats, and the one we had the longest. He was about eight weeks old when she brought him home, and the family named him Dope. Dope had his very own personality and was really misnamed, as he was quite clever. He liked to try to open the front door by turning the doorknob. If there was a chair or table near enough to the door, we would find him standing on it, leaning over, and holding the doorknob with his paws trying to turn it. I sometimes wish I had taken a picture of this, as it was funny to watch his attempts. Whenever he was outside and wanted in, he learned quickly that sitting in front of the door and meowing was fruitless, so he started his own method of "knocking." He would stand back as far from the door as possible, take a running leap high into the air, and hit the door full force. He would then slide down, and if we didn't open to him immediately, he would do it again. Sometimes we would open the door while he was still hanging on it, and that, of course, caused some laughs. But the funniest times of all were when someone just happened to be opening the door to exit, totally unaware that Dope was in his flying mode. Sometimes he would bump right into the person. Other times, he would fly into the room and fall to the floor. Fortunately this didn't happen often, as there was a huge potential for injury. I am really not a cat person, but I did become attached to Dope. He seemed to know exactly when I would arrive home from work, and he would be sitting on the windowsill watching for me. He didn't deign to come to the door to greet me; he just watched out the window to be certain I was arriving on time.

I strongly believed it was important for my children to be well rounded, so I encouraged them all from a young age to participate in as many extra curricular activities as they were interested in. When Cheryl was very young, the two girls took classes with the local city's recreation department. The classes they took were ballet and baton twirling as I recall. At this time, the classes were mostly for Coral Joy, and Cheryl was just a tag-along. Her only interest in the classes really was to be with her older sister. She didn't seem to have any particular talent for dancing at that time; however, she was very enthusiastic, as all the bumps and bruises very clearly showed. When the older children became interested in music, each playing a different instrument, Cheryl tried playing a flute, but just didn't seem to take to it. Singing wasn't an interest or specific talent for her either. Then Coral Joy became interested in acting and tried out for the local city's recreation department's current play, *The Pale Pink Dragon*, which was a story all about a beautiful princess, a wicked stepmother, and a wicked stepsister. Cheryl, as usual, tagged along with her big sister, and there was something about the theater that seemed to spark her interest much more than any of the previous activities she had participated in. Each girl earned a part in the play. Coral Joy got a lead role as the wicked stepsister, and Cheryl got the part of a dancing flower. The girls enjoyed the experience so much that they tried out for more plays. They both exhibited a great deal of talent in each of the plays they participated in. I, the proud mother, of course had dreams of stardom for both of my daughters. Coral Joy seemed to be born to acting. She just played a role as if it was a part of her. Cheryl, on the other hand, had to work harder at it than her sister, but she enjoyed the experience no less for it.

Cheryl enjoyed acting so much that she continued with these local plays even after her big sister moved on. In the beginning, Cheryl just had bit parts. After *The Pale Pink Dragon*, her next play was *Fiddler on the Roof* in which she played a village girl. The next play was *Little Moon*, in which she was dressed like a Chinese girl and came onstage to open and close the curtain. There was an unexpected twist to this play. There were two girls who performed this function. One came on from stage left, the other from stage right. In the opening-night performance, Cheryl and the other girl were feuding (for real), and they kept trying to upstage each other. It became obvious to the audience, and they laughed thinking it was part of the show. The director was not pleased with the girls at first, but like every good director, since it had a positive outcome, she left it alone. Cheryl next had a small part in *Aladdin and His Wonderful Lamp*, playing one of the sisters to the princess. After that play, there were three more plays in which she had bit parts. And then there was a play called *Snoopy and the Gang in the Far Out Wars*," in which Cheryl had a lead part. She played a very convincing Lucy. If you have ever watched any Charlie Brown cartoons, you know who Lucy is.

When the boys joined Pop Warner Football, the girls wanted to be cheerleaders for their brother's team. At that time, Gordon was living in a different city with his father, so that left George's team. The girls thought that they would be joining a cheer squad of girls and that they would learn about cheerleading, as they had never done this before. As it turned out, George was put on a sort of leftover team, and there was no cheer squad for that team. Then the girls turned to me, asking me to be the leader of the cheer squad so that they could be cheerleaders for their brother's football team. I was reluctant, as I knew nothing about cheerleading. The girls assured me they would do all the work of making up the cheers, so I agreed and signed up to be the leader. There were only four girls in my squad—my two girls and two other girls who were also sisters of a boy on the team. It was fun being the leader of this cheer squad, and since it was my first experience, I was very glad to have such a small group. I believe Cheryl and her sister were very good at cheerleading considering they were quite young and this was their first experience. They worked diligently to learn the cheers and put together the appropriate moves. Cheryl was seven years old at this time, and she was thrilled to be doing this along with her twelve-year-old sister. It was fortunate we had the circumstances we had, because if the girls had been with a large group and a different leader, they might have had less opportunity to be involved in all the cheers. I might add that such a thing would likely not even be possible today, as cheerleading has developed into a major athletic sport.

At eight years old, Cheryl wanted to become a Brownie Scout, following in the footsteps of her older siblings who had all been scouts at one time, Coral Joy being currently involved in Girl Scouts. At that time there wasn't a Brownie Scout troop near us that Cheryl could join, so the girls came to me with a request that I start a Brownie Scout troop. I had been an assistant troop leader for Coral Joy's Girl Scout troop at one time, so the girls decided that I could start a troop for Cheryl so she could become a Brownie Scout. As much as my time would allow, I made every effort to become involved in the various activities in which my children were involved, so I applied to the local Girl Scout Council and became a Brownie Scout leader. I really enjoyed this, and Cheryl had a group of special friends in the troop with her, so she also enjoyed herself. My assistant leader was the mother of one of Cheryl's closest friends, and Coral Joy served as an unofficial assistant leader as a project to earn a Girl Scout badge. I think the most fun for Cheryl was when she started going to Girl Scout camp each summer. She always came home all excited about her experiences. When she attended her first year at the Girl Scout camp, her big sister was there also. They were in different programs in different parts of the campground, but Coral Joy was able to visit her little sister to ensure all was well and help to ward off any possible homesickness. It became a summer tradition for Cheryl to attend Girl Scout camp for the next three or four years.

Since I had to spend so much time at work, when my yearly vacation rolled around, I tried to do something special with the children. When they were younger, most of our vacations involved going to Grandma and Grandpa's house or staying home and taking daytrips to places like Disneyland and Knott's Berry Farm. As they got older, however, I wanted to be more creative and give my children more enriching experiences, so I decided to take the kids camping. The girls and I had been on a few short weekend camping trips with the Girl Scouts, and we had really enjoyed it. I just knew that my sons would enjoy it as much as we did given the chance. Did I realize what I was letting myself in for? A woman alone in the wilderness with four children ages six to thirteen? Perhaps to a small degree, but it seemed as if it would be an adventure for the kids. I could take them to places where they could let off steam and learn about nature at the same time.

And so it began. I did extensive research into every aspect of camping so that our experiences would be safe and successful. First I studied what camping items to buy—tents, sleeping bags, stove, lanterns, first aid kit. I thought of these purchases as investments since they could be used more than once, and we could take camping trips each year and maybe even on some weekends. I researched what kinds of meals to prepare on camping trips, and of course I needed pans, dishes, and eating utensils. I got the girls involved in the planning and picking out of the freeze-dried food and other items. The boys were living with their father at this time, so they weren't involved with the planning as much. One weekend when my son George came over to spend some time with me, he and I read the instructions and tried to learn how to put up the large tent that I had purchased. It would sleep six to eight adults. We were doing it in my living room, so we couldn't really set it up completely, as we couldn't put the stakes into the floor the way we would put them into the ground. In any case, we sort of laid it out with all the poles in the right places to get an idea of what we would be doing when we set it up for real. We also read all the instructions on lighting the Coleman lanterns and Coleman stove. After this I was confident that we were ready to take our trip.

Now that we were all prepared, I began planning where we would go on our first family camping trip. I decided we should take a trip that summer to Canada, driving up the coast and camping along the way. The kids all thought that sounded like fun, so we began making our plans. To be fully prepared for such a grand adventure, I thought it would be wise to take a weekend camping trip—a sort of dress rehearsal to the "big trip." I decided the best place to go was to Lake Casitas, which is several hours northeast of Los Angeles. A friend of mine at work had suggested this lake to me. He said there was a nice campground, and the lake provided good fishing; he was sure the kids would really enjoy it. Our little weekend trip turned out to be quite an adventure, and it definitely helped to prepare me for what was to come on our long trip to Canada. Here I was, a young mother with four kids. We had each gone camping with Boy Scouts or Girl Scouts, but never before had we camped as a family. Never with just me in charge. And I was soon to discover that we were not as ready as I had hoped we were.

I had bought a luggage carrier for the top of the car because my little hatchback just wasn't big enough for our family and all our gear. We packed up everything, covered it all with a tarp, and then tied it all down tightly—at least as tightly as we could. I thought we had done a very good job. So we all piled into the car and set off for our adventure. When not much time had passed, we were tooling along the freeway all excited and happy about our coming weekend outing when I began hearing a thump-thump-thump! Just as I was trying to figure out what was wrong and hoping it wasn't a flat tire or anything more seriously wrong with the car, the kids—three of whom were sitting in the backseat—all began giggling. They didn't tell me why; they left it to me to figure out. Suddenly I looked to my left and saw a large portion of our bundled up gear hanging down the left side of the car and thumping against my window. Obviously we weren't as strong as we thought we were, and we hadn't tied our load down tightly enough. I got off of the freeway at the next off ramp. Fortunately we were out of the city by this time, and we found a nice side road to stop on. I asked George, who was the oldest and hopefully the strongest, to help me fix it. The tarp had started to rip from the wind that had whipped around the top of the car while we were traveling at freeway speeds. The rope had not come completely untied, but had loosened considerably, so we had to wrap up the gear again as much as was possible by tucking the ripped part of the tarp underneath it all. Then we had to tighten the rope as much as we possibly could. I believe I even pulled the rope through the windows and used them to help anchor the load down. I drove more slowly for the rest of the way to the lake. As a result, it took much longer to get there than I had planned.

When we finally arrived at the lake, it was almost sundown. It was still early in the spring, and daylight saving time had not yet begun. We found a good campsite and began unloading all our gear. Everyone was hungry, so we unloaded the food first, and I fixed dinner for the kids. I had trouble lighting the lantern, but finally got it going as dusk rapidly approached. If I were to do it all over, I would have had the kids wait to eat so I could set up the tent while it was still light out, because as it turned out, I could not figure out all the poles, and I couldn't remember all I had learned from our practice run. So George and I worked on it for quite a while, and Gordon helped also. The girls were getting tired and cranky, so I stopped working on the tent and unloaded the station wagon completely. I put their sleeping bags in the back so they could sleep there for the first night. I had bought air mattresses to put under all the sleeping bags, but I had nothing to blow them up with, so I began trying to blow them up by mouth. This was a major fiasco! I kept blowing and blowing and trying to hurry and get the mattresses ready for the girls, and they were getting colder and crankier by the minute. And then I began getting lightheaded, and I started laughing. I guess it was the lack of oxygen that made me silly, because I started laughing and I couldn't stop. I remember laughing for quite some time. The kids got the biggest kick out of my behavior, and they teased me about it for years to come. Finally I just bundled the girls up in the sleeping bags and put them down for the night in the back of the car. Then the boys and I went back to work on the tent. We managed to get it partially up. We thought it would be fine, so we got all settled in our sleeping bags for a good night's sleep, minus air mattresses as I recall. I don't remember if it happened right away or much later in the night, but the tent eventually fell down around us. I remember sticking my head out through an opening and deciding, "What the heck! We'll just sleep like this and fix it in the morning." The boys and I turned our bags around so our heads were partially outside of the tent so we could breathe, and then we settled down again.

The next day, as the kids and I walked around the campground, I looked at the other tents to see if I could get an idea of how to put ours up. The really funny thing about all of this is that when George and I had been practicing at home, I had put the instructions away somewhere, and I hadn't brought them with us. In any case, when we started putting it up the second time, it was easy, and we wondered why it had been so difficult the night before. The rest of the weekend was fun and even rather relaxing. At the end of the weekend, I felt more than ready for our big trip in the summer. I don't remember having any difficulty on the drive home, so I guess we solved the problem of the loading and tying down of the gear.

While preparing for our big trip to Canada, I bought maps and books on campsites all the way up the coast and into Canada. I noted the ones that required reservations and which ones were free and which ones charged a fee and so forth. Once again I wanted to make sure that I was prepared for every circumstance that could come up. I also continued to read up on camping. I wanted to ensure I had all the necessary gear and supplies. The one thing I had learned from our little rehearsal was to expect anything!

The time for our big adventure finally arrived, so we packed up the car, all piled in, and off we drove. Before leaving, I double-checked to be certain we had not left anything important behind. This time George and I secured our gear tightly so there would be no mishaps along the way. The planned trip was a little less than two thousand miles, which we could make in a couple of days if we were driving straight through, but this was to be a vacation with sightseeing stops along the way and overnight camping rather than staying at motels. Campgrounds were usually quite a distance off the main highway, so the timing of each day's drive had to be calculated as carefully as possible so we could complete our trip in the allotted time. Also to be considered was the fact I was doing all the driving myself, and I needed to ensure I got sufficient rest. And, of course, with four children there would be lots of bathroom and food stops. I don't remember each and every town we drove through or each place we stopped along the way, but there are some significant memories I do recall. In later years when I took trips, I would keep a journal of sorts, but it didn't occur to me on that first trip, and I did keep rather busy trying to entertain the kids in the car and trying to avoid bickering and fights and so forth. It is to be noted that this was before Game Boys, CD players, and other such mobile entertainment for young travelers. Coral Joy took along her little cassette player and two cassette tapes—Donnie Osmond, a heartthrob for preteens back then, and Three Dog Night, a popular rock group. The Donnie Osmond tape became "lost" early on in the trip, and we suspected the boys had something to do with that. When the trip was over,

I thought I would never want to hear music by Three Dog Night ever again, but now when I hear their music, memories of that trip come back to me.

All four of my children were hyperactive, and taking them on a two-thousand-mile trip was actually rather a brave stunt, a fact that I didn't fully realize at the time. We were all cooped up in the car for hours at a time, so when we stopped for the night, I found it difficult to contain them. They wanted to run and yell and act crazy. That was fine in some campgrounds, but when we were in more crowded areas with campers on all sides of us, it was a bit more of a challenge to convince them that we had to follow campground rules, and we had to be considerate of others. I remember one night we were driving through Oregon and we couldn't find a vacant campground. I saw some other people camping on a beach, so we pulled in, parked, made a campfire, and cooked our dinner. It was warm so we didn't set up our tent. We just put our sleeping bags around the campfire pit and went to sleep. As dawn was breaking, the kids were just waking up as a beach patrol drove through. An officer stopped to tell us that we were not supposed to camp overnight there. He was talking to me, and I was still lying in my sleeping bag. He said, "Tell your parents you can't sleep here overnight." We all got a kick out of that because he didn't realize I *was* the parent! We didn't say much. I just said, "Okay." After he left, we packed up, ate our breakfast, and left, which we were going to do anyway. There were several more nights when we either couldn't find a campground or they were all full and we had to "wing it," so the trip turned out to be even more of an adventure than I had expected.

When we got into Washington, we stopped to visit my sister and her family for several days before we headed on into Canada. The kids got to visit with their cousins, and we all had a good time. My sister wanted us to stay longer, but I wanted to get on the road. I wanted to get to Canada, so I promised to drop by and visit again on our way back home, and we left on the next leg of our journey.

We made it to Canada on schedule with no further mishaps, and it was beautiful. It seemed to me that the sky was bluer and the air was fresher and the trees were bigger than I had ever seen, but maybe it was just that I had never camped there before, and it was all a new experience. We had no difficulty finding the campground that I had chosen from the guidebook. It was a very large campground, and there was a beautiful lake. Luckily it was not crowded at all, and we had our pick of camping sites. I selected a site far from any of the other campers so the kids could really enjoy themselves and let off steam. And let off steam they did! We were allowed open campfires, and there were woodpiles at each campsite, so that first night I started a campfire, and the boys kept feeding it with logs and running to other vacant campsites and getting more logs. They had built a very big and high bonfire before I realized it. I had to curtail their activity as I became worried they might start a whole forest fire—that was how big the fire was! While I was preparing dinner, the girls said they needed to go to the bathroom. They didn't want to walk down the hill to the facilities, so they decided to go out in the woods. That was fine with me, and I told their brothers not to follow them but to leave them in peace. The boys were having such fun with the fire that they left their sisters alone. Soon I heard the girls screaming and saw them running out of the woods trying to pull up their pants, still screaming all the way. At first I wondered what the boys had done to them, but soon realized the boys were right where they were supposed to be. It turned out that the girls had disturbed a large wasp nest while trying to do their business, and the wasps got pretty angry and buzzed all around them. They didn't get stung, but they both got quite a scare, and the boys and I couldn't stop laughing. Kind of mean for their mom to laugh at them, but it was just so funny I really couldn't help laughing! It wouldn't have been funny if it had happened to me, of course. Needless to say, the girls walked downhill to the bathroom the rest of the time we were there.

The remainder of that evening was peaceful. After dinner we sat around the campfire, sang songs, and told stories. Then we settled down for the night all snug in our nice big tent, which we were now experts at putting up. Sometime in the middle of the night, Coral Joy woke up suddenly, very sick to her stomach. When I realized she had started to vomit, I sort of shoved her out the door of the tent so she could do it in the dirt. When she was finished, I helped her get changed and cleaned up and had the boys shovel dirt over the contents of her stomach that were now directly in front of the tent door. I congratulated myself on a catastrophe averted. Or so I thought. Cheryl had stayed inside the tent while this whole event was going on. Then, when I could finally check on her, I found her just sitting up in her sleeping bag and crying silently, big fat tears rolling down her cheeks. At first I didn't realize why she was crying until I turned on the flashlight. It was then I saw that I hadn't quite managed to get Coral Joy outside in time. She had gotten sick all over Cheryl's head because they had been sleeping side by side. Cheryl's hair was all matted and sticky. So I had to get her out of the tent and get her cleaned up as much as possible. There were water faucets in the campground, but there were no showers, so we did the best we could with what was available. After we had cleaned up the tent and Cheryl, we all went back to bed to get a little more sleep. In the morning we got up, ate breakfast, and packed up to leave. It was time to head home. The girls, especially Cheryl, didn't want to stay there anymore; it just wasn't as much fun as they thought it would be. It was too bad, as it was a beautiful and peaceful campground, and I would have loved to stay just a few more days. We probably could have toughed it out, but I guess we—especially the females—were not the tough campers we thought we were. Cheryl was only seven, and this was her first big camping experience.

So we headed south, prepared for the long trip home. Crossing over the border going into Canada had been a smooth experience; coming back into the United States posed a small challenge. We were loaded down with our camping gear, and as we waited in line for our turn to go through the border crossing, I noticed some cars were being pulled out of line, and the drivers were being asked to unpack their belongings. I was sure this was just routine, but it worried me—not because I had anything to hide, but because it had taken us so very long to get our gear all packed up just right, and if we had to take it all out and unpack it, it would take us a very long time to get it back together again. Also, the kids were all uncomfortable, especially Cheryl and Coral Joy. They were very anxious to get somewhere so they could get cleaned up. Fortunately, when it was our turn, I just had to answer some questions—like where we were going and where had we been and why we had come into Canada. Then they asked a few test questions to ensure I was telling the truth. It wasn't so bad after all. I did understand the importance of it all. As I think back, I am sure if we were doing the same thing today, it would be a bit tougher to get through the border considering all the things that have transpired in recent years. For example, passports were not required then to cross back and forth between Canada and the United States as they are now.

When we arrived back at my sister's house, we had to explain why we had cut our trip so short. I explained that now it was my intention to get us all cleaned up and then head for home. After everyone got cleaned up and we had a home-cooked meal, we felt better, so I decided to stay for a few days to visit more with the family. We celebrated my thirty-fifth birthday while we were there. My sister fixed us a nice dinner with a cake and a small celebration. Eventually we headed for home. We had a few small adventures along the way, but we made it back all in one piece. I have, however, always wondered why, when arriving home, I was not carted off in a strait jacket, or at the very least why I hadn't gone completely gray. As it turned out, that was the biggest family camping trip we ever went on. We never had another adventure in which all five of us went camping together. I never attempted to travel so far in one trip again either.

I was, however, a glutton for punishment, because in future years we continued to camp. I even began taking the kids on backpacking trips. On our very first backpacking trip, I took only the two girls. Cheryl was about eight or nine years old at the time. We found a nice place on Mount Whitney, just outside of Lone Pine, California, where we could safely park the car and hike up the mountain. That became our favorite backpacking spot, and we would return there many times. That very first trip was challenging, with many adventures for the three of us. The drive up the winding mountain road was challenging for me, and to add to that difficulty, Cheryl played on her sister's fear of heights. I told Coral Joy to sit on the floor of the car to avoid looking out the window. That way she couldn't see how high up we were. But Cheryl kept laughing, joking, and telling her sister, "Look out the window! You don't want to miss this view!" Then she'd say things like, "Wow, it sure is a long way down!" The most memorable part of that first trip was the hike back down the mountain when it was time to go home. A light snow had started to fall, which surprised us, as it was July. Cheryl began singing "Jingle Bells" and skipping and dancing. Then, when Coral Joy chimed in, she tripped and twisted her ankle. Cheryl and I found her a big stick to use as a walking stick, and we started on our way again, the girls singing all the way down the mountain, Cheryl dancing and Joy limping. But through it all, we thoroughly enjoyed ourselves, and we decided that backpacking was a lot of fun. We were determined to do it again soon.

When Cheryl was about ten years old, I decided it was time to brave backpacking again. Coral Joy wasn't interested in going this time, so I decided to invite one of Cheryl's best friends, Karen, to go along with us. Karen's mother was concerned about letting her daughter come along because she had never backpacked before, but I assured her it would be fine. I had done this before, and we would pick an easy trail and find a good, safe camping site. After much coaxing, Karen's mother finally agreed to allow her to go. We went to our favorite backpacking place. Things were going smoothly, and the girls were having a lot of fun. Then, as luck would have it, after we had been there just a few days, Karen fell and banged her arm. I didn't think it was serious, but I decided to cut our trip short anyway to take her home. As I recall, the arm was not broken or even sprained, but I still felt kind of guilty, having so strongly assured her mother that nothing bad would happen.

In the early years of our marriage, my husband and I were baptized together in the Baptist church; this was the church in which we had chosen to raise our family. The Baptist belief is that babies should be dedicated to the church by their parents, but not baptized until they are old enough to make the decision to do so for themselves. George and I had dedicated each of our children in the Baptist church when they were infants. Cheryl was about eleven years old when she made her decision to be baptized. She enjoyed going to Sunday school, she sang in the choir, and she felt a closeness to God. I was very proud of her and encouraged her as she grew in her beliefs. She also joined the Awana youth program in the church and remained active in it for a few years. At one evening ceremony, she was surprised by being presented with an award for being the most dedicated young person in her group. When the announcement was made, she was standing with the other girls at the front of the church as family and friends watched. The leader of the Awana group began explaining the award that was being given. She then described the special young lady who was about to receive it. When the leader announced "This special young lady is Cheryl Jean Beechum" it was obvious that Cheryl was surprised. Her face lit up, and she was all smiles. I do believe this was one of the most special events in her life. I was so proud of her, and I wished the rest of the family had been present at the ceremony. She frequently talked about her beliefs with me. I remember one particular discussion we had when she was about twelve years old. She and I were driving somewhere together when she suddenly exclaimed, "I just looked up and saw Jesus in the clouds, Mommy. Did you see him?" Of course I was concentrating on driving. I hadn't been looking up in the sky, so I told her that I hadn't seen anything, and she said, "I am sorry you missed him, Mommy." Events like this happened from time to time. Looking back, I have wondered if she was being prepared for her future.

5

Tween and Teen Years

As Cheryl approached her teen years, her personality was well defined. She was outgoing and friendly. She was still rough-and-tumble, but she now channeled this energy into her various activities. She was a big, healthy girl, and she was growing like a weed. At twelve years old, she was taller than her big sister, and by fourteen years old, she was gaining on her big brothers. This was when she started calling Coral Joy "my little big sister," which remained her favorite nickname for her sister from then on. At this age, she began to have problems with catching colds quite often. It seemed to me more than just the allergies that she had struggled with over the years. I discussed my concerns with the family doctor during one of Cheryl's regular checkups, and he decided that she needed to have her tonsils and her adenoids removed, as he believed that they were the cause of the worst of her symptoms. He assured us that this would help to relieve many of Cheryl's health problems. She was only twelve at the time, and she had never been in a hospital before. She was very nervous about having the surgery, but we decided that if it would relieve her misery, it would be best to do it. I stayed with her in the hospital room until they wheeled her into surgery. I waited for her and stayed with her afterward. She survived nicely and recovered quickly. She was treated well in the hospital, and whatever she feared never came to pass.

Cheryl's symptoms had been relieved somewhat by the surgery, but her allergies still seemed to be a problem, so when she was thirteen, I took her to an allergy specialist, who conducted various tests to determine exactly what she was allergic to. The results showed that she was allergic to trees, grasses, weeds, and, of course, animal dander, which we had already known. I spent all that money to find out that she basically had hay fever. For a while we visited the specialist who gave her a shot every week, and then after a time she received them only several times a month. I eventually stopped the shots because it ran into way too much money, and we began using over-the-counter medicines. For the most part, they worked fine—just as well as the shots so far as we could tell. There was one product that we used for quite a while. It was called Allergy Relief Medicine, or ARM. Cheryl and I had lots of laughs with that acronym. When her symptoms would begin, I would say, "Cheryl you are sneezing again? Where is your arm?" Cheryl and I had lots of fun with many things like that. When I was busy raising all four of my children, it seemed I was working all the time or busy with their various activities, so I had very little time to enjoy each one individually as much as I would have liked to. When they all grew older and went out on their own, I had much more time to spend with Cheryl, and I will always be grateful that I have those special times with her to remember.

Cheryl was no longer in cheerleading at this point; that had just lasted a season or two while her big brother was playing football. She was still in scouting, having bridged over into the Intermediate Girl Scouts; however, I was no longer her troop leader. She was a little lazy, especially when it came to school. It's not that she wasn't a good student; she just wasn't interested as much in the learning aspect of school as she was in the social aspect, and sitting down to do her homework was "boring," that word now being her favorite description of her life. In reality, Cheryl's life was anything but boring! I know because I was the one who had to drive her to all her various activities. When she was eleven years old, Cheryl once again showed an interest in dancing, so I enrolled her in the Patti Joy School of Dance, where she attended dance classes for quite a few years. She did quite well this time and made good progress. She took tap, jazz, and beginning ballet classes. As usual, she was very enthusiastic and put her all into her dancing. She was quite good when she performed; however, she acquired many bumps and bruises to get there. Her siblings called her Grace as an ironic nickname. While taking dancing classes, Cheryl also participated in the dance school's recitals. I have some very special memories of her dance recitals. Her teacher did feel she had talent. She told us that if Cheryl would stick with dancing, focus, and practice, she could become quite good. There is one particular recital that I remember. She may have been fourteen or fifteen; I am not sure. But it was a special dance—a solo that her teacher had choreographed just for her. Cheryl selected her own music and worked very hard on this performance. I invited all the family to attend. When she finished, she didn't think she had done very well, but in fact her performance had been outstanding!

Cheryl competed in her first beauty pageant at the age of twelve, and it came about quite by accident. Her big sister had registered for the pageant and had paid to participate, but then she was in a minor car accident in which she received a slight concussion, so she really wasn't feeling up to going onstage. Cheryl was just beginning to blossom into a beautiful young lady, so Coral Joy suggested we enter her little sister in her place. We talked it over and checked with the pageant officials, who allowed us to enter Cheryl in her sister's place so that we didn't lose our deposit. I am not sure who enjoyed this first pageant more—me, Coral Joy, or Cheryl—but I do know that this was the beginning of our involvement in the fun and excitement of the world of beauty pageants.

When Cheryl was thirteen years old, we signed her up for the Wendy Ward Charm School at the local Montgomery Ward store. It was something that her sister had done before her, and since Cheryl had competed in the beauty pageant, she had become very interested in modeling. The program culminated in a fashion show for the girls so they could show off their new skills. Her sister and I were so proud of her. She was actually very graceful up there on the stage. She wasn't the skinniest or the prettiest girl on the stage, but from the moment she walked out onto that stage, everyone noticed her.

Camping was something that Cheryl and I continued to enjoy well into her teenage years. One particularly memorable outing was a backpacking trip to our favorite backpacking location. I took my two girls along with Gordon and his best friend, Mike. We were having a very pleasant time; nobody had gotten sick or hurt so far, and no unexpected weather had descended upon us. On this trip, the girls and I were sleeping together in a small, two-man tent. It was warm and cozy, with the three of us taking up approximately the same space as two grown men would use. In the morning when I woke up, I was lying on my back. As I opened my eyes and looked up, there, inside at the top of the tent, was a spider. A big, hairy, ugly spider! My daughters and I are all staunch arachnophobes, and knowing this, I lay as still as I could, not wanting to wake the girls—or disturb the spider. As the girls awoke, they saw the spider too and looked to me for guidance. I, of course, just motioned for them to lie still. We whispered to one another, but we were afraid to move or jiggle the tent at all. We just knew that the stupid spider would fall down on one of us. The really funny part was that we knew that if we talked about it too loud, we would make the guys aware of our predicament, ensuring that they would come over to shake our tent. What a quandary we were in. Being the mother and supposedly the most composed of the three of us, I was delegated to crawl slowly out and then help the girls out before we shook the spider out of the tent. I don't remember quite how we managed to accomplish this feat, but I know that we did. As we were recovering from this event, the guys laughingly told us that they had found a dead mouse in our water bucket. They said they had considered not telling us but felt sorry for us after our "ordeal!" So they spilled the beans. As repulsive as this was to us, we knew it could have been worse, so we just got more water and boiled it over the fire before using it. We were roughing it, after all, which is what camping is all about, and by now my girls and I were experts!

As memorable as that outing was, I think that Cheryl's most memorable camping trip would have to be the trip that her Girl Scout troop took in April 1979. Cheryl was fourteen at the time, an Intermediate Girl Scout. Her troop was planning a canoe trip to earn a badge. The entire troop would be attending, and each girl was to have a parent or guardian with her. In preparation for the outing, Cheryl and I took canoe lessons with her troop. We were looking forward to this trip; we had done extensive planning and preparation. We had everything ready to go. Then at the last minute Coral Joy went into labor. This child about to be born would be the first in the next generation in our family, my first grandchild, and Cheryl's first nephew, so we were both very excited about the upcoming birth. And as babies do, this one had chosen a very inopportune moment to make his appearance. He chose Thursday, the day before we were to leave on our trip. Cheryl wanted to back out of the trip. She wanted to be there for her sister. She wanted to hold her first nephew when he was brand new. But I insisted that she go, as she had worked so very hard on the lessons. To finish the trip and earn the badge was the glory of it all. She finally relented and went on the trip without me, her leader made an exception in this instance regarding the need for a parent. She was, however, very disappointed about not being in the hospital when her very first nephew was born.

Around that time I began to worry about our cat, Dope, as his behavior was becoming erratic. He would seem to be walking around in a confused state, bumping into things. Then he began urinating in various places in the house, which he had never done before. I took him to the vet one day when all the kids were in school, and I discovered that he had feline leukemia. This was a surprise to me, as I had never before realized that cats and dogs could get what I thought were "people diseases." As it turned out, Dope's condition was very advanced, and there was no treatment, so the vet recommended we put him to sleep. I thought it over. It seemed like the right thing to do, so it was done right away. I then had the terrible task of telling my children. The older ones accepted it reasonably well, but Cheryl was quite upset, more with me than anything. She understood it was the most humane thing to do, but she felt I should have given her the chance to say good-bye to her cat. It was very painful for her to accept; she felt I had not considered her feelings at all. In retrospect, I realized she was sort of right, but I had considered her feelings. I just thought it would be easier for her not to have to be there to face the situation. I was wrong, and I truly came to regret my decision. After this I didn't want any more pets, but Cheryl loved cats so much it was hard to deny her. So, of course, not very long after that, we got another cat.

The next kitten we had was a pretty little thing—a sort of silvery gray. My elder son decided she should be named Belladonna, which we shortened to Bella. She came into our lives shortly before we were planning to move from our apartment into a house. She had just adjusted to the apartment when suddenly we moved her to a new and strange place. Cheryl and I took her with us one day when we went to check out our future home. Bella's reaction was totally unexpected; she slunk around the house and sniffed in all the corners. She seemed not to like it. I was thinking maybe the previous renters had cats or dogs, and she was wary of their scents. In any case, the minute she could snatch an opportunity, she zipped out the back door, across the yard, across the street, and over the high brick wall of a neighbor's house. Cheryl was hot on her heels, but alas was too late. Bella had scaled the wall so quickly no one could have caught her. Much to our chagrin, she leaped right into the jaws of two large dogs. We couldn't see what was happening, but we could hear it. She was too young to have learned how to escape such a situation, and the dogs thought this was a wonderful plaything that had jumped into their midst. I believe they were tossing her back and forth. In a heartbeat Cheryl was over that six-foot wall. To this day I have no idea how she did it. Just adrenaline I guess. She punched one of the dogs in the nose, grabbed Bella, and handed her over the fence to me. It was so sad holding that nearly lifeless little body. Cheryl climbed back over the fence, and we jumped in the car and took off. But the odds were against us. We were new to the neighborhood, and it was Sunday. When we finally located a veterinarian's office, it was closed. Poor Cheryl stood there for ten minutes banging on the door to no avail. Finally I convinced her we needed to return home. She cried all the way home as poor little Bella breathed her last, dying in Cheryl's arms. The next day I called Animal Control for dead animal pickup. Since I was at work, Cheryl waited for the pickup. She had placed Bella tenderly in a small shoebox as her casket. She told me when the officer arrived she too had cried to see such a beautiful little kitty, lifeless.

Some time later Cheryl insisted on talking to the owner of the dogs. She kept saying she hated them and wanted the owner to know what his dogs had done, even though I told her they were not really vicious; they were just doing what came naturally for them. They were not killers; they were just playing with this little kitty. There was no evidence that Bella had been bitten. There had been no broken skin and no blood. I am sure they just broke her neck while bouncing her back and forth like a little toy. When we visited the neighbor, he came to the door with his dogs. One of them whined and backed away quickly when he saw Cheryl. The man wanted to know what my daughter had done to his dogs. Cheryl explained that she had punched the dog right on his nose. It could have been funny if it weren't so frightening. These were large dogs, and I kept thinking how they could have attacked her. The fact that they didn't was proof that they weren't vicious.

Even this traumatic experience didn't deter Cheryl from wanting another cat, and soon after that Bright Eyes came into our lives. This cat had beautiful coloring and looked a bit like the

American Wirehair, which is a breed I have recently researched. Cheryl found him as a stray and fell in love with him immediately. She always said he reminded her of Dope even though he was sort of marble colored while Dope had been all gray. And Bright Eyes had much longer fur. He was a bit of a wanderer; he would be with us for a few days. Then he'd disappear for a few days before returning. Cheryl did some investigating and discovered that, on the days he was not at home, he was visiting a neighbor woman. He never went into her house, but he stayed in a nearby tree, and she put out food for him on her porch. It was funny because she thought he was a stray. When Cheryl was planning to go to Florida to visit her dad, she asked the neighbor if she would take care of Bright Eyes, and the neighbor agreed. But when Cheryl returned home from her trip, Bright Eyes had disappeared. We didn't see him anymore. He never came back to our house, but the neighbor said that she saw him from time to time. She even fed him every once in a while. She said he looked healthy and well cared for, so he must have found a home he liked better.

When Cheryl was fourteen years old, she decided that she wanted to go live with her father, who now lived in Florida. Her siblings tried to talk her out of it; their father had remarried and had a new family now. They had experienced what it was like to live there for themselves, and they assured her she would be miserable. Her dad was trying to encourage her to live with him. He was making all kinds of promises, as was his habit. Her siblings had already experienced the fact that he was not a person to keep his promises. They told her how unhappy she would be, but she was determined to go. One day Cheryl came to me in tears because they were trying so hard to dissuade her. I told her that they were just concerned for her, but she was adamant. She had to follow her heart. I told her siblings to let her make her own decision; she was old enough to do that now.

So off Cheryl went to live with her father in Florida. She went with high hopes, but she did not have a long-range plan. Perhaps she was thinking she would stay there until she graduated from high school. I don't know if she had plans further into her future at this time in her life. She tried hard to make it work, but within six months of living with her father and his new family, she was ready to return home. Her father mostly wanted her to babysit for the children of his new wife, and help with chores around the house. He did not sign her up for dance classes or Girl Scouts as he had promised, so she quickly became disenchanted. Her brother George, who lived close by during that time, was a big help to her. Having lived with his father recently, he knew what she was going through. He would visit her often and spend time with her to cheer her up. She would always be grateful to him for doing that for her. When she finally called me, brokenhearted, saying that she'd had enough and wanted to come home, I arranged for her to return as soon as possible. Upon her return home, she was so upset about the entire situation, she said she didn't want to speak with her father ever again. Cheryl never fully reconciled with her father. As it turned out, they both died young before having a chance to work things out. There was one attempt by her siblings to get Cheryl to reconcile with her father. He had been diagnosed with leukemia when he was forty-five years old; he made a trip to California from Florida specifically to see his children one last time before he died. Cheryl wasn't ready to reconcile, but grudgingly went along with the family reunion. She just seemed relieved when it was over.

When Cheryl returned home from Florida, everything returned to normal pretty quickly. She was so grateful to be back.

Cheryl and I returned to our regular routine. She went to school. I worked and drove Cheryl to all her activities.

Shortly after she returned, at a regular dental checkup, the dentist suggested that Cheryl get braces. I wasn't surprised, as I had been through this with my other children; crooked teeth did run in the family. This didn't bother Cheryl at all, especially since she was beginning to get seriously involved in dancing and acting at this time. In those days braces were worn for about a year and, of course, it required some special care of one's teeth. I needed to stay on top of this situation. As I have mentioned, Cheryl was a bit lazy, so she didn't always follow through on the proper brushing of her teeth. It did pay off in the long run, as her teeth were quite beautiful when the braces were finally removed.

In her younger teen years, Cheryl babysat on a few occasions to earn extra money. She loved children and was really very good with them. But babysitting didn't pay a lot, so she embarked upon other endeavors. When she was about fifteen, she went to work for a fast food restaurant. Since she was still in school, it was necessary that she have a work permit; the school required a student to have good grades before issuing a permit. Her grades were acceptable, so there was no problem with that. Working at this particular fast food place did, however, become a problem. California imposes some very strict regulations on businesses that hire teenagers, and rightfully so. The regulation that immediately impacted Cheryl was that young people were not allowed to work past ten at night. Her schedule began after school at around four or five. She and several other young people were scheduled to work until closing at ten. Then, after closing, they were required to clean up before they could leave. This entailed putting food away; cleaning tables, chairs, and counters; and sweeping as well as scrubbing and mopping the restrooms. When the evenings were not busy, they were able to leave within the hour after closing, but many nights I sat in the parking lot waiting for Cheryl for two or more hours after closing. This made it difficult for her to get up for school the next morning, and she often had difficulty completing any necessary homework. I was upset. I wanted to file a complaint, but Cheryl insisted that if I did, she and her friends would lose their jobs, and it might mean that this place would not hire young people again. So I complied with her wishes until a bigger problem arose.

Her supervisor began sexually harassing her. He offered to give her better assignments and better working hours if she would "be nice to him." He asked her out, and she declined. Suddenly she was fired. He trumped up some story about how she didn't do her job efficiently. At this point, I did get into the picture. I wrote a letter of complaint to the district manager, who scheduled a meeting with Cheryl and me. Of course he brought the supervisor to the meeting, and he, naturally, blatantly denied each accusation. Cheryl looked him straight in the eye as she recounted the incidents that had transpired, so I was convinced that she was telling the truth. I threatened to take the complaint to a higher level. I think the district manager believed her also, because he then offered Cheryl a job at a different store within his district. He said she was a good worker, and he didn't want to lose her. (*So why was she fired?* I wondered.) I told him, "No way." I didn't want her working for that company anywhere or in any capacity. All we really wanted at this point was an apology, which never happened.

6

The Young Woman

By the time Cheryl was sixteen years old, she was well on her way to becoming a young woman. I could see in her the woman she would become. Her siblings were grown and on their own, so she and I had much more time together even though I was still working. She became very busy and had a lot of activities. Until she was old enough to drive, I drove her everywhere, and this gave us the opportunity to talk and laugh together.

I remember several disappointments that Cheryl experienced during this time in her life. Being a very sensitive person, she took them quite hard.

One year a local shopping mall held a contest near Mother's Day. People were asked to write a short essay about how special their mothers were, and Cheryl wrote something to submit. I don't recall what the prize was, but it was important for her to tell people how much she loved me and why. I was not aware of this, as Gordon took her to the mall. They walked around for a very long time, but for some reason were unable to locate exactly where to enter her submission. When she came home, she was in tears, and it took me quite a while to get her to tell me what was wrong. I tried to comfort her by telling her how much I appreciated the thought, even though it hadn't worked out as she had hoped.

On another occasion, I had to comfort her in much the same way. She tried to give me a surprise birthday party. She was about seventeen at the time. She made up nice little invitations, took them to my office, and gave them to several of the people I worked with. She even printed RSVP on them. Unfortunately, no one showed up, and only one person responded. This was a secretary in the office, and she gave Cheryl a gift for me. Cheryl had bought snacks and drinks and had me get all dressed as if we were going out to dinner. She wasn't quite sure how to explain to me that we were actually sitting and waiting for guests, but as it turned out, we waited in vain. When no one came, she broke down and told me what she had planned. Then she got angry, and finally, of course, she cried. It was difficult explaining to her that people are sometimes very thoughtless. I tried to tell her not to let it get to her. I suggested we go out anyway, but she was too upset, so we just stayed home and enjoyed the snacks she had prepared.

It was about this time that Cheryl brought home a cat named Princess. Princess would end up being Cheryl's last pet. She looked very much like Bright Eyes, whom Cheryl still missed very much. But it turned out that Princess was a loving cat who did not wander, and she became attached to Cheryl very quickly. We were nervous when it came time to move into the mobile home I had just bought. Cats don't always take well to a move as we had learned once before. But as it turned out, our worrying was for nothing. Princess settled into the new place very well. When Cheryl died, Princess mourned for her. I had never experienced such a thing before even though I had heard of pets mourning. I would have kept her, but she would roam around the house looking for Cheryl, and when we boxed up Cheryl's clothes and things, Princess would lie on the boxes and sleep. She sometimes tried to open the box to get inside as if she wanted to cuddle in Cheryl's clothes. Coral Joy, who helped me box up Cheryl's things, put the boxes into a closet, but Princess would find a way to get in there and sleep on them. She seemed so sad I finally decided it might be better for her to have a change of environment, so I gave her to Gordon, who was happy to have Princess around in memory of his little sister.

The mobile home that I bought was located in Gardena, California, and Cheryl attended Gardena High School. Gardena was a racially diverse community, and on occasion unpleasant situations resulted from this. The school, therefore, offered a workshop titled Brotherhood USA. Cheryl participated in this program and was given an opportunity to attend a Brotherhood Camp. She felt this was very worthwhile. She made some new friends, and she learned some helpful information. Still, Cheryl was becoming more and more unhappy with school and was threatening to quit altogether, so I sat her down, and we had a talk about it. I made an agreement with her that I would permit her to quit school if she would take and pass the GED test and thus get her high school diploma and then go on to junior college. She agreed to this. As soon as she passed the test, she enrolled in Harbor Junior College. She was very pleased about that, as it made her feel that she was grown up now and working toward her future. She decided to major in fashion design. She took fashion design, modern dance, and beginning acting classes.

Since Cheryl was majoring in fashion design, she was given an opportunity to spend some time at the LA Fashion Mart, located in the fashion district in downtown Los Angeles. The Fashion Mart holds designer shows several times a year, and the young women from the college had the chance to participate by helping the models dress. Cheryl participated in two shows and really enjoyed this opportunity. It inspired her to start drawing some dress designs. The decision to major in fashion design had been a good one because it gave her a different perspective on the fashion world other than just modeling.

Besides going to school, Cheryl continued to participate in dance classes, theater, and beauty pageants. As well as the modern dance class she was taking at the junior collage, she participated in two summer dance workshops with the Al Gilbert Dance Studio in Hollywood. She always said she wanted to be a professional dancer, but she didn't really have the drive to practice, practice, practice, as was necessary to improve her skills to the level of professional. She did, however, have a love of dance and a lot of enthusiasm, so she stuck with it.

All the beauty pageants that Cheryl competed in were based in California. There were local competitions, state competitions, and national competitions. Many of the national competitions were held in Las Vegas. After the beauty pageant in which Cheryl took her sister's place, she didn't compete in another one until 1981. She entered two or three pageants that year and really began learning the ropes. In some of these early pageants, she wanted her big sister to come along and help her dress and fix her hair and give her moral support. In those days she felt more comfortable with her sister backstage than she did with me. Coral Joy came whenever she was able to, as by this time she was a young mother of two, and she was busy with her own family. In 1982 Cheryl participated in six pageants. There were two pageant systems, the Delta Queen System and the Sunflower Miss System. She also took part in the Miss Gardena Loyalty Day Pageant and the Miss South Bay Pageant, which was a preliminary to the Miss California Pageant System.

By 1983 she had become quite an accomplished pageant participant and had won many titles. That year she participated in eleven pageants. She continued in the Delta Queen and Sunflower Miss systems as well as the Miss Gardena Loyalty Day Pageant and the Miss South Bay Pageant. She also discovered the Skipperette Pageant, the Miss Palos Verdes/San Pedro Pageant and the Miss Carson Pageant. In the Delta Queen and Sunflower Miss systems, she won or placed in the following categories; Bathing Beauty, Miss Congeniality, Most Photogenic, Best Personality in a Photo, Model of the Year, first place in Royale Miss Dramatics, and fourth alternate in Sunflower Miss Talent.

Whenever we walked into a room to register for a pageant, Cheryl was always dressed in her best. I recall watching the other girls looking at her with envy as if they felt she would be difficult to beat. Cheryl had a lovely, outgoing personality. She always enjoyed herself whether she won or not. She always took one or two other girls under her wing and tried to help them. She often picked out a girl who was new to competing and gave her pointers about how to behave and how to carry herself. Once or twice the girls she helped actually won. She made several close friends this way. One might think that she would refrain from helping others so she would have a better chance of winning, but that wasn't her nature. She just continued to be the same outgoing, friendly, helpful person that she had always been.

In 1983, a special award was created by the woman who ran the Sunflower Miss Pageant. It was at the nationals for this pageant, and a breakfast had been arranged for all contestants and their families on the last day. The major awards had already been presented the previous evening at the final dinner gala, but a few last awards were being presented at the breakfast. After the presentations, Micki, the woman who ran the entire pageant, began a speech about how she enjoyed working with the young girls and boys and the young women. She said that, every once in a while, a young woman would stand out in the group. She spoke of a young woman who had been participating in her pageant system for the past few years. She indicated this young lady was very special and had a wonderful, outgoing personality. She talked about how happy this young woman always seemed to be, win or lose. She went on with the praise for a few moments and then explained that she had felt it appropriate to create a special award, which she was calling "Miss Amity" because the young woman was more friendly, kindhearted, and affectionate than was traditionally necessary to receive the Miss Congeniality award. As she finished, she announced that the first recipient for this new award was Cheryl Jean Beechum. Both Cheryl and I sat there sort of in shock—or surprise! I was the first to realize what had just been announced, but Cheryl still just sat there. Now everyone was clapping and looking at her, so I gave her a nudge. She finally gathered herself together and went up to be crowned and get her trophy and banner. Then I ran up to hug her and knocked her crown off! It was quite an exciting event. The year following Cheryl's death, the award was renamed the Cheryl Beechum Award in honor of Cheryl and what she had brought to that pageant system.

During these pageant years, Cheryl and I became really close. We shopped for special clothes and planned which pageants would be best for her to enter and what categories she should participate in. We practiced her talent together. We laughed and played around just like sisters at times. She would teach me some of the latest dance moves. I was really a poor dancer, but we laughed, and I kept trying. We sang together, and one of our favorite songs was "You and Me against the World." We developed a signal between us. When she was onstage, she would look for me in the audience and unobtrusively put her little finger to the side of her nose, just briefly. And I would return the signal. This was sort of our sign of "good luck" or "I love you."

At one of her pageants she did a monologue for her talent entry, and everyone really enjoyed it. Later in the weekend, there was a talent event for the mothers. They were to try to perform the talent their daughters had done. I really didn't like getting up in public, but I surprised Cheryl by signing up for this event. I did her monologue. I had memorized it because I had helped her practice it over and over. I didn't perform it as well as she did, of course. I watched her in the audience as I was performing, and she had her hands over her eyes. I thought she was embarrassed or even that she was laughing at me, but later I learned, from the friend she was sitting with, that she was trying not to cry. That told me she was quite emotional about it.

In 1984 she participated in only two pageants since we had talked it over and decided it was time for her to move on. By now other things were beginning to happen for her. She was attending junior college studying fashion design, and taking beginning acting classes, so we discussed the possibility of finding an agent for her. We then found the Alese Marshall Institute of Fashion and Modeling, and we signed her up. She began studying self-improvement and fashion, speech dynamics, TV commercial workshop, advanced visual poise, interview techniques, and photographic modeling.

In April 1984 she auditioned for a part in a production put on by the Irvine Community Theatre, called *You Know I Can't Hear*

You When the Water's Running. The production consisted of four short plays; she got parts in two of them. She played a secretary in *The Shock of Recognition*, and she played a blonde bombshell in *The Footsteps of Doves*. She was very convincing in this part. She enjoyed acting even though she learned it could be hard work. I believed she had a future in this field. She also worked as an extra in a movie called *Passions* and volunteered to do a part in a training film for the Los Angeles Police Department.

Being in beauty pageants was quite expensive. Entry fees, money for special dresses, and sometimes traveling expenses added up quickly. Cheryl knew it was costing me a lot of money and really wanted to help pay her own way. So interspersed among school and all her activities, she also had a variety of jobs.

At sixteen years old, Cheryl got another job at a fast food restaurant, and her experience there was much more pleasant than it had been at her previous position. I don't remember how long she worked there, but I do remember that one of the young men she worked with became her boyfriend for a while. At some point she worked as a Candy Striper at Torrance Memorial Hospital. This, of course, is a volunteer position, but it was good experience for her, and she enjoyed it very much. She also found a job in a nearby shopping mall at a dress store. I don't recall the name of it, but it was a nice place, and she enjoyed selling. She worked there for only a few months because she had difficulty meeting her quota. It was not a problem with selling; she enjoyed that, and she was very helpful to the customers. But she was also very honest. If an outfit didn't look right on a customer, she would say so. If the store didn't have what the customer was looking for, she would send her somewhere else rather than push something that was not wanted. The unfortunate part was that the other salesgirls would be pushier and sell more, but many of their items would be returned. Cheryl prided herself on the fact that everything she sold stayed sold; she had no returns. The sales staff worked on commission, but returns were not deducted from commissions or quotas. That seems quite unfair, but that is the business world. Anyway, she was let go because she didn't meet her quota. It was a harsh lesson to learn, and she decided she couldn't do this type of work because it wasn't in her to be dishonest.

When Cheryl was a little girl she always said that when she grew up, she wanted to be a traffic officer just like her mommy. That made me feel good, but I didn't really think she was serious. I knew her interests would change as she became her own person, and for the most part, I was right as her interests turned to acting, modeling, and the fashion world, but an opportunity came along that she didn't want to pass up. In my role with the Los Angeles Police Department, I was involved in the training of new officers in all aspects of the job. I trained them in writing citations and impounding vehicles as well as in professional demeanor. I also developed a traffic control training program that had not existed before. Sometimes other agencies would contact us in search of someone to help them with a training program, and I sometimes would be recommended for that assignment. When a small California seaside city was looking for someone to assist them in developing a pilot traffic officer program, my supervisor recommended me. I was given a work permit to work, on my own time, for this other city. When I helped them create the program and they began a process to hire temporary officers, Cheryl wanted to apply. So I gave her permission but said she would be on her own; I would not pull any strings or insist that she be hired. Her training in the pageant systems came in handy here as she was very good in job interviews. She also knew a lot about my job and was able to answer questions with a great deal of knowledge and potential. She was hired and attended the training program I was running; she was even able to help me in the classroom with demonstrations. I was proud of how much she had learned from me by just paying attention to things I had discussed at home about my work.

She truly enjoyed this job, and I was quite proud of her progress. The assignment was facilitating traffic movement in the evenings as people were leaving work and heading home. The intersections covered were on a main street leaving the city going toward the freeway. The city had been experiencing serious traffic slowdowns when everyone left work at the same time, making the progress toward the freeway painfully slow. The pilot program was initiated to determine if traffic control could assist the movement of this exiting traffic. The city felt it would be more cost effective than installing traffic signals at each intersection, especially due to the fact that traffic control was not needed at any other time of the day. There was one issue on which the police department disagreed with me. In Los Angeles we had learned many years earlier that the use of flashlights to direct traffic flow after dark was not safe as it often confused the drivers. Much more effective were white hats, white gloves, and reflective safety vests along with the use of specific, understandable hand signals. These tools made the officers visible when the vehicle headlights shone on them. Well, the city insisted on issuing flashlights and wanted me to instruct officers on their use in directing the drivers' movements. As I continued the training, I did my best to provide instruction in the safe use of flashlights.

One evening there was an accident at the intersection where Cheryl was working. No one was injured, but there was damage to two vehicles. The woman, who had driven against traffic and against the direction Cheryl had given her to stop, blamed it on the traffic direction. She said the flashlight had confused her, and she thought the signal meant for her to go when actually she was supposed to stop. Without going into great detail here, I will just say that, since this was a new circumstance to the police department in this city, the accident report was not written correctly. For example, instead of identifying Cheryl as a traffic officer, they called her a pedestrian. A few days later the woman driver decided to sue the city. The city attorney determined that it would be best for the city to accept liability and to fire the concerned officer (Cheryl). I felt responsible for this in a way, as I had caved in to the city's demand to use flashlights. They did give Cheryl a hearing before letting her go, and the lieutenant who sat on the review board told me she was very poised and handled herself very well, but they still decided to go with the recommendation of the city attorney. I also met with them and even had a meeting with the city attorney. I told them that if they accepted the liability, they were setting a precedent for any future accidents that might occur in an intersection covered by an officer directing traffic. My input fell on deaf ears, and I was certain this was a case in which my being her mother was a hindrance. I believed they did not pay attention to my logic; rather, they thought of me as just a mother fighting on behalf of her daughter, when in fact I would have defended any of the officers in a similar situation. This was unfortunate, and I decided that my job there was finished. I had done the training, and it was their decision whether or not to continue the program. I never learned what was finally done. Meanwhile, Cheryl was crushed, as she had been so proud of this accomplishment and truly believed the accident had not been her fault. I reinforced that belief for her. And life went on.

While searching for another permanent position, Cheryl tried selling Princess House crystal as well as Empress Pearls. She would give crystal parties and pearl parties, which was really fun but didn't bring in a lot of money. Next she tried selling Vorverk Vacuum Cleaners. She enjoyed this and tried very hard at it. She went into people's homes to demonstrate the vacuum and was so enthusiastic and excited about the product she would surely have been successful eventually. She didn't quit this job; she was still on their payroll when she had her accident. The last job she had was with a customs brokerage. The wife of a police officer friend of mine hired her as a messenger and sort of "gofer." She was impressed with Cheryl's work ethic, and this had the potential of becoming a permanent job. She was working and on her lunch break the day of the accident. She had left the office to go to the bank to take care of some personal business. Everyone at her office was concerned when she didn't return to work; a few hours later, they learned of her accident. I hadn't thought to call them. As it was, I was having a difficult time right then even thinking straight. I never did find out who called her office to inform them of her accident.

CHERYL JEAN BEECHUM "BUG"
MAR. 3, 1965 — AUG. 29, 1984

7

Saying Good-Bye

I sat with Cheryl for as long as possible while I revisited the past. After a while, the doctor came in and asked to speak with me. We walked out into the hallway where Joy joined us. The doctor was a neurologist and the primary doctor on Cheryl's case. He said that he was going out of town for a few days, and he wanted to let us know and give us the name of the doctor who would be filling in for him. He didn't have much to tell us about Cheryl's progress, or lack of it. We learned later that this doctor always had difficulty telling family members bad news.

After the doctor left us, we were sitting in the waiting room once again, which was beginning to feel sort of like a second home we had been there so long. A short time later, the new doctor arrived and asked to speak with us. Joy and I met him in the hallway. This doctor was very straightforward—almost blunt—in telling us that there were no longer any brainwaves. There hadn't been for a day. Essentially, Cheryl was gone. He suggested we give permission to unplug the machines, especially if we wanted to donate organs so they would still be fresh enough to use. I had been trying to prepare myself for this event, so, sadly, I gave my permission. Joy and I just stood there in that hospital hallway holding each other and crying. I remember seeing a young man out of the corner of my eye who had started to approach us, but then he stopped. Cheryl's friends had been coming to visit throughout the week, and this was another one. She'd had so many. I am sure he could sense what was happening and was considerate enough to hold back. I never knew who that considerate young man was.

At this point all I can say is "Thank God for my other three children." They were my biggest support during this time, along with my mom. My sister flew in from Washington, and my friends at the police department also stood by ready to help. My children worked with Ralph, a friend from the police department, and found a mortuary and funeral home and arranged for the funeral. They chose Utter McKinley Mortuary in Downey. They arranged for services to be held at Memory Garden Memorial Park in Brea, California. This was a bit far away, but they offered special rates to members of the Los Angeles Police Department. The funeral was to take place on September 5, and my family and my friends made all the arrangements.

I decided on a closed casket because of the head injuries that Cheryl had sustained, and all her beautiful long blonde hair had been shaved off. She just didn't look like Cheryl. I wanted to remember her as she had been, and I wanted the same for her family and friends. We had a beautiful photograph of her placed beside the casket. It had been taken by a friend from work who was an amateur photographer. Cheryl had posed for him on a few occasions, and we had used several of his photos for her portfolio.

He had enlarged a beautiful head-and-shoulders shot and had it put in a nice frame. He gave that to me, and I have it to this day hanging in my home. The funeral home was overflowing with Cheryl's friends as well as friends of mine from the Los Angeles Police Department. The family was driven to the services in a limousine as per custom.

We were able to get the minister from the church that Cheryl had attended in Redondo Beach when she was younger, the same church in which she had been baptized. He just barely remembered her, but his wife seemed to remember her very well. A friend of mine from work provided some music; actually, he played the guitar and sang. He had known Cheryl from a young age, and he felt badly about her loss. The family, including Mom, Jolita (my sister), George, Gordon, Coral Joy, and I, sat in a small alcove in the front of the chapel. It was semiprivate, and after the services people came to us to offer their condolences. Since we were having her cremated, there would be no graveside services.

When the services were finished and we were back in the limousine, my other three children and I opened a bottle of champagne and toasted our precious Cheryl. She really would have loved that. Then the family, along with a few close friends, were invited to the home of the aunt of Cheryl's very close friend, Diana. Cheryl was well loved by Diana and her aunt; they had spent lots of time together. As is tradition after a funeral, there was a lot of food, but I don't recall being able to eat much, if anything at all. I remember very little about the rest of the day except for a conversation with Diana's grandma, who had liked Cheryl very much. She said to me, "It was so sad that she had this accident, and you always made her take her vitamins." That sort of made me smile because the vitamins had nothing to do with the accident, and yet the reference to them seemed to have been important to this lady. What it said to me was that Cheryl talked about me and what I had expected of her. Many people I spoke with then and for weeks afterward told me how much Cheryl loved me and how often she spoke of me. Even the guys that she had dated told me this! That was nice to hear. I remember one young man who was there. He hugged me and cried on my shoulder. He was a simple guy who had been very much in love with Cheryl. I think she had cared a lot for him, too, but had she lived, I don't believe she would have married him even though he had given her a lovely engagement ring. She had a habit of taking people—both guys and girls—under her wing to help them out, and this was just another one of those guys. I returned to him the lovely diamond ring he had given her.

A few days after the funeral, I visited the site of the accident. I couldn't help but relive the event, wondering how it must have been for Cheryl. The only consolation I have is that I don't believe she knew what hit her. The police were never able to get a statement because she was unconscious at the scene. Although the accident was legally considered her fault, I always thought the other driver felt some sort of responsibility because, even though he had been slightly injured, he never sued me. He never even had his insurance company contact me, and he never filed a claim with my insurance company. Someone—maybe the police officer— had gathered up several items, including papers that had fallen from both cars during the accident. I was given a large plastic bag full of these items. Even though it was difficult, I eventually went through them all, and I found many papers that belonged to the other driver, so I mailed them to him. I still never heard from him—not even an acknowledgement that he received the papers I sent to him. I will never know how he felt about the accident.

Meanwhile, I was puzzled that Cheryl had not applied the brakes at all. I began thinking that perhaps something had been wrong with the car. I had recently had the car checked, including the brakes, and supposedly all was fine. I consulted with a lawyer to see if I had a case. I didn't really want anything in particular, like money, but I thought that if there was some issue with the Mazda being faulty, my investigation might be helpful in preventing future problems for anyone else. The lawyer said it would be difficult to fight a large automobile company, but he would do some investigating. I think he did this more to ease my mind than anything else. His firm did have the car thoroughly checked, and after a few weeks I received a letter advising me that, in their opinion, I did not have a case. The letter also stated that if I chose to pursue the issue further, I could contact another law firm. I chose not to do so. I never received a bill for their services.

8

Grieving

Now it was time to lay Cheryl to rest and to begin the grieving process. I needed some time away from home and work, so I went up to Salinas to my mom's soon after the services. George stayed behind, and when Cheryl's urn was ready, he picked it up and brought it to Salinas. I purchased a plot in the Garden of Memories Memorial Park in Salinas where my father, my brother, and other family members were interred. It was a regular-sized plot that could hold more than one urn. I also purchased a headstone large enough for the engraving of five names. My original thought was that my four children and I would all someday be interred there together. Now, however, my remaining three children have their own families, and thus their own future plans. Years later, I had Mom's urn interred there, and someday my urn will also be laid to rest with Cheryl. We had a small family gathering at the grave site. Most of the family members in attendance were those who had been unable to attend the funeral in Southern

California. Funerals are supposed to help give some closure. I am sure in many cases they do, but I don't think the closure came then for me.

My life was pretty much upside down for a long time to come. I had bills to deal with, insurance companies to deal with, and my own grief to deal with, unfortunately in that order. The hospital bill was over $44,000 for just one week. Then there were all the extras as well as the various doctor bills. Initially my medical insurance refused payment. It seems that Cheryl was no longer eligible to be insured under my policy from the time she had turned eighteen. She had been nineteen and a half at the time of the accident. I argued that no one had told me about the age restriction, and yet they had still accepted my premium payments (and probably would have for years to come if this had not happened). I read over the policy and learned that she should have been eligible because she was attending junior college. I guess it was my responsibility to have notified them, although the policy wasn't specific on this score. I presented my case and heard no more for a while. When I finally received a call saying my claim was still denied I yelled at the woman on the phone, "Forget it now! She is dead!" I slammed the phone down. Within the hour, I received a call back saying that the claim would be honored after all.

Meanwhile, other events were transpiring. I had applied on Cheryl's behalf to Medi-Cal and subsequently was approved; my friends and coworkers had taken up a collection that amounted to a couple thousand dollars, and when I began receiving the various doctor bills, most of them posted their billing amount with a notice that they would accept whatever the insurance covered. All of these things went a long way toward relieving my financial concerns. Also my car insurance company was just great.

They classified the car as totaled and covered everything, even arranging to handle all the legal details of having the car junked.

Spending time with Mom helped me somewhat. There was no forgetting, however. Everything I saw, every song I heard, everywhere I went, something reminded me of Cheryl. I even saw Cheryl everywhere—driving down the street, standing on a street corner, shopping in a store. This really was a strange sensation. I cried a lot even though I am normally not a crying sort of person. I sat and read every sympathy card, and I sent thank-you notes for each card and each donation of flowers and money. There were even some donations to hospitals and church funds. It was painful to write to each person, yet it was a sort of catharsis. It was at this time that I learned the full extent of Cheryl's involvement in Sunday school and church programs. There were so many of her friends from church who sent well wishes and sympathy cards. I had known she had many friends, and yet it was still amazing as well as comforting to see how loved she had been.

When Mom asked me to go to Hawaii with her for a short vacation, I cried because Cheryl had wanted very much to go to Hawaii and was hoping to do so after she graduated from college. At first I really didn't want to go, but Mom finally convinced me. I tried to enjoy myself and tried not to act all mopey and sad, but it was mostly an act. My brother, Bob, and his son, Skye, lived there on the Big Island; we stayed with them. We were there over Thanksgiving and visited the Volcano House for a Thanksgiving buffet dinner. As I recall, there was a lot of food, but I didn't really enjoy it much. For many months after losing Cheryl, I ate only because I had to. Food tasted mostly like cardboard or nothing at all. That was a first for me; in the past, food had always been a way of providing comfort when I was unhappy or sad, but not this time.

Upon returning home from the trip to Hawaii, I returned to work and began to immerse myself in order to forget or at least bury the pain in the background. Fortunately, there were major changes happening in my workplace. Due to these changes, I was able to get completely lost in my job. I worked long hours whenever possible because going home to an empty house was very unpleasant. Coral Joy had packed up Cheryl's things because I just couldn't deal with them yet. She didn't remove the boxes—just put them all in a closet. No one wanted to part with Cheryl's things just yet. As I mentioned, the kitty Princess missed Cheryl very badly. She would sit on piles of her clothes until they were packed. Then she would sit on the boxes in the closet. It was at this time I decided to give her to Gordon, hoping to relieve her grief.

Then I made a major decision. I decided to sell the mobile home—the last place Cheryl and I had lived together. I wanted to move away. When I began looking for a house to buy, a friend at work told me that the cities in San Bernardino County were growing. He suggested I look at the many model homes that were going up there. I subsequently purchased a home and sold the mobile home. Then my daughter, Coral Joy, and her family moved back to California and came to live with me for a while. It helped me to have my two grandsons around; our home came alive again.

I am aware that, in some families, when a young person dies, no one speaks of that person ever again. Perhaps it is hoped this will erase the pain. Personally, I felt that talking about Cheryl would help us to cope with her loss. Keeping her memory alive was less painful than letting her slide into obscurity. I didn't really want to put her on a pedestal, but I did want this family to remember her. Geoffrey, my younger grandson, was so young that he didn't really remember Cheryl. He was cute and bubbly and loved to be the center of attention. So it just seemed natural that when Geoffrey was four years old, we entered him in a beauty pageant. He had blonde curly hair and a cute little chubby face. He turned out to be a natural. He enjoyed walking onstage and developed a love affair with the camera. He also felt attracted to the microphone and easily spoke into it whenever onstage. The very first pageant he competed in he won! He was still young and a bit bewildered about it all, but he had fun with it. Coral Joy and I felt very nostalgic and also a little sad the day of the pageant, this being the first one we had participated in since we'd lost Cheryl. The best part of that day happened when we went out into the parking lot to take pictures. Geoffrey still had his little tuxedo on, and we stood him beside the two trophies he had won. While my son-in-law was taking his pictures, Coral Joy and I stood back and watched. We looked at each other, and one of us said, "If only Cheryl could be here now, she would be so proud of him." Suddenly, to our amazement, Geoffrey struck a pose that we had never seen him do before, and have not seem him do since. He put his right index finger on the top of his head. With his left hand, he poked his stomach, and he stuck his tongue out. Coral Joy and I were shocked. We just hugged each other and cried. You see, this is the exact pose that Cheryl used to strike when she was a small child. The similarity between the two of them was amazing. They both were chubby with curly blond hair, and both had that sparkling personality. Geoffrey had never seen Cheryl do this, of course, and had no way of knowing what Coral Joy and I were positive of—that this was a sign from our dear Cheryl saying, "I am here watching, and I am happy." That was the one and only sign that we have ever had from her. But to this day, Coral Joy insists that Cheryl is Geoffrey's guardian angel.

I have discovered there really is no time limit on grief. It is just a process each of us must work through. Each person is different;

each loss is different. Some parents who lose a child are able to work through it by creating some type of memorial or fund or program to help others. I, however, did not have any ideas or the resources to begin such a project.

Now that many years have passed, I have decided to go through old boxes of Cheryl's things—old pictures, cards, letters, and school papers. I am reading a lot of things and learning more about my daughter. I thought I knew her. I did know part of her, but through my reading, I am learning more details than I ever knew before. Not all that I am reading pleases me; some of it makes me feel I should have been closer to her, should have talked to her more and been there for her more, but it is way too late to cry over that spilled milk.

Cheryl saved many of the letters she received from friends over the years, and since I have been in touch with two of her closest friends, I decided to return their letters to them. They both expressed appreciation for the opportunity to travel down memory lane for a while.

9

Cheryl's Final Gift

Cheryl embraced life, and she loved people. She always wanted to reach out and help people, so donating her organs when she passed was the ultimate gift. She had talked about donating her organs when she was quite young. She was a devout Christian, and she loved helping people. It never occurred to either her or myself that this decision to donate was to be thrust upon the family much sooner than anticipated. While she was lying in the hospital's trauma center close to death, of course my prayers were always that she would live, but as the days passed and it began to be obvious that we would soon lose her, I decided to tell the head nurse to relate this decision about organ donation to the proper person.

When the accident turned my life upside down, the decision to donate was comforting rather than painful because I knew I was following her wishes and I knew this would perhaps help another family who might be suffering the potential loss of a loved one who was in need of a vital, life-giving organ.

The accident had happened on a Monday, and she was in a coma until Wednesday, when she came out of it for a while. I brought all the family together, and we prayed and expressed our love and tried to bring her back to us. We finally lost her on Friday. It was a painful week, but in retrospect I have come to believe that week was a gift to us from God, an opportunity to say good-bye. Once we told hospital personnel of Cheryl's desire to donate her organs, we indicated we wanted any healthy organs as well as eyes, bone marrow, skin, and any other body part to be put to good use. We would have her cremated afterward. Since this had been Cheryl's wish, I could not have done differently if I had wanted to.

When the doctor told us that Cheryl's brain waves had stopped and a decision was necessary regarding removing the machines, I advised him to go ahead and "pull the plug." (It sounds so cold and sad, but it was necessary.) I was taken into a private room where a specialist explained the entire process to me. I was so numb at this point, it was difficult to concentrate, but I forced myself to listen and try to understand. There were papers to be signed, and while this was happening Joy was in the room with Cheryl watching the removal of the machines and then walking through the hospital corridors to the operating room with her. She felt the need to be with her sister and say her final good-bye. I was not really aware of this at the time, but after the fact, I have often thought how difficult this must have been for her, as she loved her sister so dearly.

As I mentioned, we had a local funeral service with a closed casket, and we planned a cremation with the urn to be interred in Salinas where she had been born. Much later, after the funeral, while we were trying to get some order back in our lives, we received a letter from St. Vincent's Medical Center where some of Cheryl's organs had been sent for transplant. The letter explained very lovingly and beautifully the circumstances surrounding the use of Cheryl's kidneys (with no names of the recipients). We learned that, because of her kidneys, there were two women whose lives had been prolonged and enhanced. One woman was young and just starting life, and the other woman was a mother with a large family. The letter closed with this statement: "I hope that the weeks since Cheryl's untimely death have begun the healing process necessary after the loss of a loved one. I, along with all the members of our transplant team, send my sympathies and thanks to you all. The recipients of your good deed extend their deepest gratitude for this most precious gift. I hope that time will bring you the peace and happiness that you deserve." This was signed by the transplant coordinator. In the midst of our tears and pain, this gave us more solace than I can ever express.

My son, Gordon, who had previously voiced disgust at organ transplants and was adamantly against organ donations after death, was really touched and perhaps the most comforted by this letter. He had been so moved he wanted to be the one to read the letter aloud at the services that we held when we had her urn interred. Not long after this, he signed an organ donor card, something he had previously refused to do.

Unfortunately, we were never told where any of the other organs were used, but I know how great the demand is for organs, and I am certain they were as helpful as the kidneys were. I have always wondered why the recipient's names are not shared with donor families, but eventually I learned that this is done to protect the donor family as well as the recipient. Should the organ subsequently be rejected, and should the recipient not survive as a result, it could be devastating to the donor family as it would almost be like losing the loved one a second time. It was really most comforting to go on believing that Cheryl did not die in vain, and a part of her lived on in another life.

I have heard people share concerns that if they told the hospital of wishes to donate organs, the fact might hasten the end of life for the patient. Doctors take oaths to do their best to enhance life, so I don't believe this happens. In Cheryl's case, I must admit that her head injuries were such that she was doomed from the start. Every effort was made by a wonderful and caring medical team to keep her alive, and the fact that we told them of her desire to be a donor did not hasten her demise in any way.

A few weeks after Cheryl's funeral, a newspaper reporter contacted me to ask if I would be willing to talk with him about organ donations. The hospital had given him my name. This is how I remember it, but it is possible that the hospital contacted me for permission to give out my name, which seems more likely. In any event, I did meet with him. He was doing a series on organ donations and wanted a donor family's perspective. I answered all his questions, and he wrote a very sensitive and helpful piece. Printing an article like this was a good idea because organ donation was not really a popular idea back then, and his story really examined the concept from both sides—the donors and the receivers. He quoted me as saying, "It all seemed so senseless. We had to try to make sense of it all." I also remember telling him, "Cheryl was a very giving person in life, so it is only natural that she would be giving in death."

To this very day when I am asked, "How did you deal with the loss of a daughter?" I tell people that the donation of her organs gave me great comfort and made it a bit easier to move on.

I want Cheryl's gift to mean something. Let it be a reminder that our lives and our bodies are precious gifts from God. When God recalls us to His side, the legacy we leave behind can be a legacy of life.

10

Memories of Cheryl

The quality of a person's life can be measured in many ways. Some measure it in years; some measure it in actions. Cheryl wasn't allowed many years in this life, but she made the most of the years she did live. Everyone who knew and loved Cheryl remembers her in a different way. She impacted many lives, and I wanted to include the thoughts and feelings of family and friends to show how they felt about Cheryl and how she impacted their lives. This is the measure of Cheryl's life.

Family

George Beechum

I think I was about seven or eight years old when Cheryl was born. I really don't remember much about her childhood until she was about seven. My memories are of the family things that we all did together, such as camping trips and so forth. I left home to live with my grandma when I was about fifteen, so I missed being with Cheryl until a few years later.

She was about thirteen or fourteen when she went to live with our dad in Florida. He had remarried, and she missed him and wanted to live with him. Unfortunately, her vision of being with him was not the same as his. There was friction from the start. Dad's new wife really didn't want us kids in his life. I don't know all that Cheryl went through, but I know it became unbearable for her. Since I was living on my own in Florida then, she would contact me whenever she could. This was before the days of cell phones, so she couldn't reach me as often as she would have liked. She cried a lot whenever we did have the opportunity to talk. Finally she had all she could take, and then she contacted Mom, who stepped in and sent her a plane ticket. I went to rescue her from Dad's, and the rescue turned into Dad taking us to the airport. Just before she boarded the plane, we hugged and kissed and said good-bye, and then she turned and left without a word to Dad. I know this hurt him.

I didn't see Cheryl again until I returned to California about four years later. She had grown up. She wasn't a little girl anymore, and I didn't care for some of her new friends. She had grown into a young woman and was beginning to find herself. I knew she would have become successful because she wouldn't have given up until she was. I am sure there would be scars; this world does that to us. I like to believe it was God's mercy to take her home early. I really miss her.

Gordon Beechum

There's so much of her I've tried not to think about. The feelings that come out still hurt.

We shared something special. She always pushed me. She knew I was able to do more with my life and myself. She never made me feel dumb because my younger sis was better than I was. The last time I remember her pushing me was to get out of bed after my appendectomy. She came to Monterey in the middle of the night from LA. I woke up after the operation and was extremely hungry. She made sure that I got the bacon and eggs I love. However, instead of having the staff bring the food to me, she made them leave it down the hall so I would have to get out of bed and walk. No matter what, she would not let them bring me food in my room.

I remember her love of cats. I remember driving her to her Awana meetings on Sunday mornings. She truly enjoyed those meetings, and it was a pleasure for me to be a part of that.

I miss her so much!

Coral Joy Beechum Parks

When Cheryl was born, I was four and a half years old. I remember thinking how nice my mother was to give me my very own living baby doll. Cheryl made it really easy for me to pretend I was her mommy. She was such a happy, amenable baby. As a toddler, she was a chubby blonde imp who was always trying to keep up with her older siblings. I could always get her to let me read to her. As she got older, one of our favorite activities was playing school. I, of course, was always the teacher. As a result of our games, Cheryl could write her name in cursive when she began kindergarten, an accomplishment of ours that I am proud of to this day. Cheryl and I spent hundreds of happy childhood hours together playing school, playing with Barbies, singing, and dancing. Because we were four and a half years apart in age, our lives eventually began to go in different directions, but we still stayed close. As the years passed, we had a typical sisterly relationship—sometimes best friends, sometimes worst enemies, always rivals in one way or another. The saddest part of losing my little sister was losing my lifelong best friend.

Cheryl's greatest impact on my life was her death. From a young age, I knew about the accident that would take Cheryl's life. It's not about believing in psychic abilities for me; it is just a fact of my life. At the age of twelve I began having a recurring dream in which I experienced a car accident from the driver's point of view. Every time I had this dream, I awoke knowing that I, as the driver, had died in the accident. This dream became such a part of my life that I was convinced I was seeing my own death. The accident in my dream was exactly the accident that took Cheryl's life. I had the dream for the last time the night before her accident. I have never had that dream since that night. It's hard to acknowledge that when I heard about the accident, I knew Cheryl would die. For some reason, I was allowed to see my little sister's destiny, and it is something I have struggled with. I can only guess I was given the knowledge to help our family cope with the tragedy of her death. Any lingering guilt should be alleviated by the knowledge that her accident and death were predestined.

When Cheryl died, I was twenty-four years old, and I remember I had so many emotions that they threatened to overwhelm me. Most of all I felt robbed! I had been robbed of that special relationship that only sisters can have. Now, with the perspective of time, I can see that I didn't lose Cheryl. God just chose a different place for her in our family.

Childhood Friends

Pandora Lemons

It was a true walk down memory lane to read the letters you sent that Cheryl had kept. I had really forgotten how much we wrote to each other! We did remain the closest of the four of us for many years after I left California. We talked a lot on the phone and really got each other through some of the challenging teen years. She was such a special person, so strong, afraid of nothing. I remember her ability to give everything to a situation she thought was worthy. I think back to when she was doing her dancing and modeling and how fearless she was. She fought for what she believed in and convinced everyone around her to do the same. She stood up for the underdog and always had your back.

We got each other through so many hard times and were the first one each of us called to celebrate something. I remember lots of conversations from Florida when she was staying there with her dad. We talked through my folks' divorce, school challenges, and everything in between. She was such a true person. I think we were much alike in that way. She never held back when she didn't agree with something, and she let you know why. In that last year or so, that became a challenge for us. I didn't hold back either about how I felt about some of her choices, and it came between us. What I thought was a break for us turned out to be the end of our relationship because she died before we were able to repair it. It was a sadness I carried for many years.

Considering she left this world so young, she definitely left a lasting impression, touching so many lives in her young years with her passion and kind heart. It was not only her external beauty that touched people. There aren't many days that go by that I don't think about her and where she would be now. Every life event I have had brings her smile to mind. I am grateful to have had the time with her that I had.

I think a lot about how lucky we both were to have had such supportive parents in those days. I was allowed to go and stay with Cheryl a lot, and she was able to come here to Seattle. My friends here loved Cheryl's visits—she was such a whirlwind to them ... so city wise! LOL

Karen Pernisco-Spiecher

Cheryl was one of my first friends. We met at Lincoln Elementary School and became fast friends. Our moms were our Girl Scout leaders, and so we became Brownies together and then Girl Scouts. Cheryl and I would go to summer camp with the Girl Scouts of Greater Los Angeles, and we would make friends with other girls, some of whom we remained friends with for many years.

Cheryl and I were inseparable. We were either at school together, involved in Girl Scout activities, or at one of our homes—so much that at times we argued with each other just like sisters. Later on we became involved in the youth theater, and Cheryl and I were in a few plays together.

One of my favorite memories was when Mrs. Beechum took Cheryl and me on a backpacking trip in the High Sierras. I believe it was in May, and the place we hiked to was covered in snow. Although I had spent a lot of time in the snow-covered mountains of California, I was always in a cabin with heat and running water. I had also at that point in my life done a fair amount of hiking, but nothing had prepared me for being on the snow-covered mountain with no heat. We could not have a fire, to my recollections because of the threat of avalanches, and I remember eating spaghetti cold. As cold as I was, it was a great memory for me—one woman and two preteen girls in the wild mountains in California with no one else in sight.

I loved Cheryl intensely, as did my mother. To her, Cheryl was another one of her children. Cheryl's death affected my mother and me, and it is something I have carried in my heart my entire life. When she passed, I was in the military and couldn't return to California, but my mom was there. At every milestone in my life I felt that I had a responsibility to experience that moment reverently, as Cheryl did not have that opportunity. There have been a million moments in my life when I have wondered what Cheryl would have done at that juncture of life, and there have been times that I felt guilt that she did not have the opportunity to grow into adulthood.

One thing I do know is that Cheryl would have been a fiercely independent and strong woman who loved her family and friends and who was as beautiful on the outside as she was in her soul.

Blanche Bulham Freeman

"Tweetle de dee, tweetel dee, dee, dee, she rocked in a treetop all day long waiting for that bird come'n to sing his song—rockin robin oh rockin robin come sing me that song tonight." Every time I hear this song, I think of you and the good times we shared.

I must say I think of us girls together a lot these days, and one day we will all continue our friendship in heaven and play silly little tricks on each other, tell our corny jokes, and laugh together again.

Sympathy Cards

A friend of mine from work sent me a sympathy card in which she made this statement: "My heart is aching for you, old friend. It's a measure of Cheryl's contribution to our lives that I can't think of her without smiling. Her warmth and enthusiasm were infectious. I hope your memories of her goodness will bring you comfort."

One of Cheryl's Sunday school teachers sent a card stating, "I wish to express my heartfelt sympathy to you and your family in the loss of your beloved daughter, Cheryl. I loved her from the day I met her and will always remember her sweet personality."

An adult friend of Cheryl's, whom I had not met (the connection was possibly through church) sent me a nice long letter and stated the following about Cheryl: "Your daughter loved and cared about you more than anyone or anything in this world. There was never a time that I saw her that she didn't have something good to say about her mom. She was so appreciative of you."

The love that came from all of these friends and family members helped me to ultimately find closure.

Printed in the United States
By Bookmasters